A Subjective Approach to International Relations

A Subjective Approach to International Relations

The Battle for Meaning

Bertrand Badie

Translated by Andrew Brown

polity

Originally published in French as *Pour une approche subjective des relations internationelles. La bataille du sens* © Odile Jacob, 2023

This English edition © Polity Press, 2025

Polity Press
65 Bridge Street
Cambridge CB2 1UR, UK

Polity Press
111 River Street
Hoboken, NJ 07030, USA

All rights reserved. Except for the quotation of short passages for the purpose of criticism and review, no part of this publication may be reproduced, stored in a retrieval system or transmitted, in any form or by any means, electronic, mechanical, photocopying, recording or otherwise, without the prior permission of the publisher.

ISBN-13: 978-1-5095-6708-9 – hardback
ISBN-13: 978-1-5095-6709-6 – paperback

A catalogue record for this book is available from the British Library.

Library of Congress Control Number: 2024945535

Typeset in 11 on 14 pt Sabon by
Cheshire Typesetting Ltd, Cuddington, Cheshire
Printed and bound in Great Britain by CPI Group (UK) Ltd, Croydon

The publisher has used its best endeavours to ensure that the URLs for external websites referred to in this book are correct and active at the time of going to press. However, the publisher has no responsibility for the websites and can make no guarantee that a site will remain live or that the content is or will remain appropriate.

Every effort has been made to trace all copyright holders, but if any have been overlooked the publisher will be pleased to include any necessary credits in any subsequent reprint or edition.

For further information on Polity, visit our website:
politybooks.com

Contents

Preface vii

Introduction 1

1 **The Return of Geopolitics: A Nostalgic Illusion or a Recurrent Error?** 16
    The foundational times of geopolitics 18
    Is geopolitics outdated? 22
    Geographic renewal 25

2 **The Two International Scenes and Their Multiple Meanings** 29
    A short subjective history of the international arena 30
    The semantic ambiguity of the international system: the perpetual conflict of meaning 36
    The two systems: the system in theory and the system in practice 40

Contents

3 Four Questions That Have Become Fundamental   44
   The identity of the actor is no longer a simple
      question   45
   Thinking about the 'Other'   51
   The construction of the context   55
   What fusion of horizons?   59

4 Rethinking the International Agenda   63
   The unavoidable battle for recognition   64
   The confusion of contexts   71
   Diplomacy has many meanings   74
   The semantic clash of powers   77

A Tentative Conclusion: The Looming Battles for Meaning   81

Notes   85

Preface

Last year, with my publisher's encouragement, I published a work that did not conform to academic routine. For the first time, I wrote a first-person narrative, an 'ego-history' that retraced the trajectory of my family and the way in which it had gradually settled into biculturality.[1] Alternately depicting the sufferings and the happy times, the joys and sorrows, the benefits and drawbacks of this condition – one that is becoming more commonplace with globalization – I explained how my personal history had very early on led me to fall into the seething cauldron of international relations. Indeed, by telling the story of this adventure, I realized that the line between the international and the national, the social and the individual, often faded away and lost its traditional impermeability.

By swapping notes with my readers, who had sometimes had similar experiences, I saw that this ego-history led directly to essential epistemological questions, questions that were often considered to be settled once and for all, but now, due to several significant contemporary events, have moved back centre stage. One example is the part played by personal experience in the discovery of the transformations affecting the world: it is far from certain that submitting solely to the supposedly objective laws of a pre-constructed geopolitics makes it any easier to solve the riddles of the present. And it is doubtful whether we gain any lucidity by looking at this world as external to ourselves, as made up of some mysterious substance quite inaccessible to our own personal judgement. Subjective knowledge at least has the virtue of transparency and honesty, but it also helps to lay bare and then overcome the postulates heedlessly constructed by other people, postulates that hold us captive.

This is only the beginning of a journey, because grasping my own subjectivity inevitably involves me taking into account and analysing carefully the subjectivity of the other people, both prominent and more modest, whom I observe. The illuminations of biculturalism encourage us, *inter alia*, to reconsider a number of apparent certainties about otherness, to access the diversity of the perceptions and constructions of reality that fundamentally characterizes our globalized world – often disconcertingly so. This is the focus of my new book. It certainly investigates the subjectivity of the analyst; but also, and even more, it investigates the subjectivity of the actors who make up the world as it is, the formidable interweaving of the understandings and – especially – the inevitably inimical misunderstandings of which the world is made, the recurrent failure to know and recognize the Other: in a word, the absence of any reference to humanity as a whole, since we unfortunately prefer ready-made geometries learned from geopolitical textbooks. If we can achieve objectivity, it is

Preface

only by fully mastering this diversity of understandings that comprises the international sphere. This, it seems to me, is the main research project for international relations, a project that this book aims to present – in a concise manner, as it is more of a road map than the story of a completed journey.

The human dimension has been relegated to the domain of utopia or morality, even though it is the only essential and truly concrete part of the international sphere. That dimension is what gives it meaning, what makes it evolve, at a speed greater than that of the strategist. Marginalizing the human element has always been the best way to yield imperceptibly to the now absolute rules of power relations as reflected in fragile statistics or quite simply by the prejudices we harbour. At a time when these prejudices are being challenged, in Ukraine, in Africa and elsewhere, humanism is regaining its share of empirical truth – even though the limited freedom that effectively challenges structures is far from angelic and can serve the best *and* the worst causes. Behind every instrument of power, there is always a human being – wise or crazy – who decides. This is also what my ego-history has taught me: the 'care bears' and the 'cuddle bears' are not necessarily where we think they are.

Introduction

There is common talk, in these times troubled by the Russo-Ukrainian conflict, of an 'alliance' between Beijing and Moscow, with its banal rationality luring them into a self-evident strategic rapprochement consistent with centuries of European history. The historical moment that we are currently experiencing is undoubtedly complex and difficult to describe, but it is unwise to depend on the simple words of everyday language: we forget that the Middle Kingdom, throughout its millennia of history, has never really gone in for alliances, and that Xi Jinping probably did not learn anything from Montesquieu or Carl Schmitt, and certainly relies on completely different reference points that need to be deciphered carefully. Our grammar is not his; and, faced with this globalized conflict – perhaps the first to register so clearly in the mysterious process of globalization – everyone, in Beijing, in Riyadh, in Dakar, in Brasilia, in Warsaw and in London, has their own reading of this Eastern European tragedy that is revealing sometimes enormous gulfs. In it, we find contrasts attributable

Introduction

to the psychological orientations of each individual decision-maker (Putin is not Gorbachev) but also to the weight of cultures, histories, and recent or past social experiences, as well as to the humiliations suffered in a more or less distant past. In another part of the world, the Sahel conflict certainly does not have the same meaning in French political and diplomatic circles as it does in the villages of Mali and Burkina Faso.

In short, the international sphere is first and foremost human, only subsequently fitting into a pre-established universal model: it is even sometimes 'too human' – subject, for better or for worse, to arbitrary and often random choices, to unexpected individual decisions as well as to the twists and turns of collective consciousness, to interpretation, to the meaning that everyone endeavours to ascribe to it. Hobbes's overly mechanical analysis is being undermined, in a way that discomfits the thinkers he has influenced for so many generations; and it is being especially challenged today by the extreme plurality on which globalization draws.

It must be said, however, that international relations during the times of European hegemony and the marginalization of other peoples were dominated by the significant – but simple – importance of the shared world of 'others of their own kind' (*entre-soi*), that strange ambience where, within an almost homogeneous space, the associate and the close rival, today's friend and tomorrow's intimate enemy, have always rubbed shoulders. Alone in the world in their mentality and their practices, European actors at that time shared the same culture, the same God, and even the same religion: when they quarrelled over this last, it was only to discuss reforms to it or the modes of its political use. They

Introduction

often spoke the same language, even though French was the universal language of diplomats: Richard von Metternich, the son of the illustrious Austrian chancellor and ambassador to Paris, made only three mistakes in Mérimée's famous dictation, while Napoleon III, the monarch to whom he was accredited, made seventy-five![1] Princes[2] were cousins and often enjoyed time together: their opposition, their tensions and their wars resembled truly consensual tournaments in terms of the meaning they conveyed, perhaps akin to 'international board games'. They did not always like each other, but they respected each other and did not seek to humiliate each other; after all, they were similar, they sought to be 'part of the same world', and they thought in a substantially identical way.

Under these conditions, any understanding between them was limited to grasping the *strategic intentions* and measuring the *determination* of their counterparts rather than the deep meaning that the latter gave to the things of the world, since this remained homogeneous. In this period, cunning and force did all the work and shaped foreign policies on a daily basis. To take up the famous distinction drawn by the German philosopher Friedrich Schleiermacher, one might say that knowledge of the Other could be limited to mobilizing the benefits of an almost routine, fully self-conscious intuition.[3] It was a golden age for strategy and therefore for 'strategists': and yet, the element of subjectivity was already there, however discrete, limited to the interpretation of the strategy carefully developed by one's rivals, who observed the same rules of the game.

During this 'Westphalian' period, from the eponymous peace (1648) to the Cold War and the dawn of

Introduction

decolonization, only Russia had a somewhat ambiguous status, as Pyotr Chaadayev had already pointed out at the beginning of the nineteenth century.[4] This ambiguity triggered an endless quarrel in the empire of the tsars, driven more by the first stirrings of social unrest and ideological polemics than by geography and mute maps: Russia was neither really inside nor really outside a Europe that only grudgingly offered it the privilege of being 'one of us' (*entre soi*). The 'Third Rome', as it was proclaimed in the reign of Ivan III – who had married the last heiress of the Eastern Roman Empire – paid Europe back in its own coin. Unfortunately, we know how tragically permanent this ambiguity was to be.

Today, the international 'game' is no longer the same: it is becoming a much more subtle process, aiming at a much more complex mutual understanding, an uncertain faculty of deciphering the attitude of actors who face us in a world that now has no limits, where so many lines are blurred. In these new times, the subjective realm is triumphing more than ever, asserting its ascendancy over ready-made data, in particular supposedly geopolitical determinants and commonplaces of every kind that set up 'imperial vocations' or 'dictatorial DNA' as the fateful subjects of history. This kind of fatalistic view gets bogged down when the world becomes more complex and when national groups and social dynamics of all kinds freely start to assert themselves. Yesterday's objective laws are artificially revived or definitively extinguished depending on choices and contexts, as are the policies that result from them.

We thus enter, as a direct result, into the unprecedented and scabrous mazes of 'international understanding', with the inevitable recourse to a demanding and rein-

Introduction

vigorated hermeneutics – a science of interpretation that took root precisely in the nineteenth century, when the world began to expand, and when the effort to understand the Other, now more distant, became an urgent but not always fully recognized necessity. This acute need to decipher actors external to us and their behaviour is now a necessary step, not only to attain a grasp of international relations but also and above all to practise them. Acting on the international scene now requires understanding *in depth* what the 'Other' is, how others see the world and themselves, what motivates them, what drives them, what shocks or reassures them, what has created their specific histories, sufferings and expectations. These various precautions, secondary or neglected yesterday, have become essential today. International relations have become an incredible *battle for meaning* – a battle that the European world (an idea now commonly expanded to include the whole West) has the greatest difficulty in fighting, accustomed as it was to being 'alone in the world', to building its relationships and its conflicts on the resemblance between rivals more than on true otherness.

The process involved has become complex because it is not based solely on cultural differences, those that come spontaneously to mind. Certainly, globalization goes hand in hand with a *cultural fragmentation* that deprives actors of a unique, universally shared code, which leads to many diplomatic blunders and above all to a tragic lack of knowledge. But things are made even worse because mutual understanding also comes up against the *dissonance of rationalities*, a phenomenon that is also growing and becoming familiar in these times of globalization. The politico-military rationality of the past, which dominated and even organized international relations all by itself, is now being replaced by an interweaving of economic, social, technological and religious software that all actors now tend to use alternately, thus confusing messages that once seemed easy to decipher.

We obviously have in mind here the way in which today's China is combining, in a complex way, its politico-strategic rivalry with the United States and an activism that nourishes its trade with the same partner, to the point of making 2022 a record year in this area, with Chinese imports soaring to more than $500 billion. But we must also remember the Sino-Japanese tensions that coexist with privileged economic ties: China has been Japan's main trading partner since 2004, and the first outlet for the latter's exports, even ahead of the United States. It is really important to bear in mind that the volume of trade between Beijing and Seoul is fifty times greater than that between China and Pyongyang – not to mention the strange partnership between Riyadh and Moscow, with its whiff of oil. Attraction and repulsion intertwine in an uncontrolled and largely neglected semantic chaos.

The supreme paradox emerges when we consider that the complexity of the world and its inclusiveness are also creating a profound and lasting inequality between states aware that they are no longer playing 'in the same category' and thus seek *respect*, *rank* and *status* even more than mere material parity. The feverish quest for these symbolic goods, intimately linked to self-esteem, is in turn becoming the banal and persistent source of a lack of understanding that is aggravated and even dramatized unless it is identified and, even more, controlled. Gestures, etiquette and protocol thus assume a major importance in relations between the North and the South, real compass points that constantly reorient not only the postures of local rulers but also the social behaviour of the populations concerned, who are inevitably sensitive to differences in meaning. The president of the Democratic Republic of the Congo, Félix Tshisekedi, pointed out to his French counterpart in March 2023 that speaking ironically of 'African-style compromise' when commenting on the elections taking place in Africa constituted 'a way of seeing things [that] must change in our relations ... with the West', as it contrasted sharply with the entirely euphemized meaning given to 'electoral irregularities' when they affected Europe or the United States. Here, words create a perilous gap in understanding, and symbols erase realism and build mistrust. This gives rise to many international vices.

These new requirements are all the more decisive as they can take an unexpected turn when they are not completely grasped. Remember Emmanuel Macron's trip to Ouagadougou, the capital of Burkina Faso, at the end of November 2017: it sought to be an emblematic occasion by initiating a real break, with particular focus on the abandonment of the notorious 'Françafrique'.[5] To demonstrate his determination clearly, the French president deployed a variety of symbols. Addressing young Burkinabe at the university, he paid tribute to Thomas Sankara, the mysteriously assassinated nationalist hero, and announced the restitution of works of art formerly removed from their African heritage, loudly proclaiming that 'the African heritage cannot appear only in private collections and European museums.' But

Introduction

when, amid the blazing heat, the president of Burkina Faso, Roch Marc Kaboré, stood up from his seat, Macron spontaneously quipped: 'He's off to fix the air conditioning!' The message was suddenly reversed: the difference in rank, signified by the use of irony towards an institution, became apparent, and the audience immediately wondered whether the French president would have said the same thing of Angela Merkel or Donald Trump . . .

These dissonances – which cover many other areas – are taking a remarkable turn compared to a time when the game involved only princes, whoever they were: the irruption of societies and a variety of actors from all walks of social life has made the phenomenon more noticeable and tangible, giving perceptions an even more important role, challenging the simplicity of the strategic thinking of yesteryear, and going far beyond questions of rank and etiquette. In February 2022, Vladimir Putin chose to launch an old-style war of conquest, having simply weighed up the strengths of the gladiators: he seriously underestimated the determination of Ukrainian society to put up a fight, as well as the very strong meaning that it gave to that fight and the resilience that would result from it, outfacing the raw effect of power. He was an autocrat unable to manage these social parameters and the subjectivity which they bore: in this case, he blithely confused the Stalingrad of 1942, the Prague of 1968 and the Kyiv of today, without taking into account the mediations of meaning that had, in the intervening period, developed within the different populations.

This battlefield of signs is increasingly turbulent and menacing. As a result, the function of understanding

Introduction

is gaining a complexity that it did not have yesterday, since the distant Other was once quite simply ignored, anonymized and then cynically enslaved, while the similar and close 'Other' disappeared under the trappings of the sole prince-strategist, often a kinsman, who confronted his opponent in a posture of quite unambiguous meaning. Today, this subtle 'mutual understanding' is central to the challenges to the diplomatic art, which aims precisely to manage separations much more cryptic than in the past.[6] It certainly explains the threat posed by the resultant risk of humiliation, a risk that arises from a paroxysmal separation,[7] but it also explains all the other dangers arising from a facile and erroneous 'translation' of the expectations of those involved. Such dangers arise from a lack of attention both to what the Other says and to the reasons why he formulates his thoughts in a way whose subtlety often escapes us: behind this frequently overlooked mystery lie two fundamental variables that the specialist in international affairs needs to grasp.

The first variable is the distinct meaning that each history has given to words or categories of thought that seem to be commonplace but whose self-evidence is misleading: 'war' and 'peace' do not have the same historical significance in Europe, in China and in Africa, since the last two have been informed neither by Hobbes nor by Clausewitz.[8] The second variable relates to the way in which politics has been woven over the centuries in each social space: we need to accept, as a determining parameter, the fact that history has long given Islam a political status very different from that which Christianity had won in Europe. In this case, the 'universal reason' sometimes invoked is quite irrelevant, since the differences operate between one religion

Introduction

coming from within society and another from outside, between one world which experienced domination and another that suffered it, between one that invented the modern nation and a third party that has never ceased to question how importing such a nation into its space can be made consistent with its own history.

In its time, the constructivist approach successfully posed some of these questions in opposition to the then dominant realist theory, but perhaps, right from the start, it focused too exclusively on the constitutive role of interests and identities, somewhat neglecting the importance of the battle over signs, statuses and registers.[9] Constructivism was an attempt to react, in a very timely manner, to the excess of objectification specific to classical theory, rightly insisting on the fact that actors are not the passive relays of structures beyond their control. Beyond this advantage, one should emphasize here the symbolic force of social interactions that are multiplying dramatically with globalization, and the political cacophony that seems to dominate the international order composed of actors undergoing the same upheavals while giving them different meanings, and at the same time associating them with antagonistic fears that are ipso facto likely to lead to war. The complex effect of images thus replaces any simple gauging of power.

This pressing interpretive need, which faces analysts and of course participants, now places *hermeneutics* at the centre of the analysis of international relations. The art of interpretation becomes a determining element in scientific knowledge. But we obviously need to go further: hermeneutics originally aimed at the interpretation of texts; beyond such an objective, this exercise of

Introduction

interpretation must now apply just as much to political decisions and to the countless social consequences that derive from them, reaching individuals (eight billion people), creating a clash of psychological and social reactions, and in turn spreading across the most diverse fields of the global game, making and remaking a context that obviously does not have the same meaning for everyone. We are far from the simplicity of the geopolitics of yesteryear, but we are fully engaged in the subtle game of globalization.

It is clear that the Russo-Ukrainian conflict is no longer just the clash of two armies as it would have been essentially in the past, at the time of the Livonian War, but a hodgepodge of different meanings, combining those created by neighbouring or rival states, by the societies concerned, by the surrounding states and peoples, and then by those from around the world, all of whom are authentically involved and anxious – but for completely other reasons that lead all of them to perceive the conflict from an entirely different perspective. This major event does not have the same meaning in France, Senegal, China and Turkey, nor of course in Kyiv, Moscow and Bakhmut – not to mention the fact that this war ultimately pervades, in a very particular way, each sector of human life (economics, culture, food, etc.), over and above its sole military dimension, thus giving rise to countless equally diverse interpretations. Likewise, the Sahelian conflict is in no way limited to a frontal clash between armies and bands of armed men but constitutes a complex field of meanings and expectations borne by a set of culturally and socially very varied actors – political classes, the residents of hungry villages, the victims of raids, desertification

Introduction

and predation, mafia networks, self-defence militias, intercommunal tensions, and so on.

This need to go out to encounter protagonists and their mode of understanding has its own aim. It is not intended to 'excuse' anyone, as a former French prime minister asserted in a frivolous and polemical manner. Discovering and interpreting a dysfunction, a danger or a pathology has never been a way of excusing those responsible but, rather, a way of treating them better. Does a doctor excuse cancer when he or she seeks to understand its development? The real objective is political, in the strong sense of this word, one that touches on the very constitution of a sustainable politics: to find a potential way of reconciling meanings, perhaps even the 'sympathy of souls' of which Victor Hugo spoke, transcending these different paths, or at least the 'thought of thought' posited by Aristotle, the common denominator of a humanity destined to live together around a common codification, or even the 'fusion of horizons' that the German philosopher Hans-Georg Gadamer put forward in his popularizing of the new hermeneutics.[10]

Such a fusion does not necessarily mean consensus or mutual approval but simply the minimal understanding, the exact grasp of what the other means. For centuries, this objective was limited to the modest level of cities and tribes; it then became more demanding and spread to empires and nations: today, in less than half a century, it concerns the world in its entirety, giving it a dizzying dimension less easy to master but more decisive than ever. International relations have had to transform themselves, moving from the modest science of 'geopolitical' transactions between states to an understanding

Introduction

of the close and delicate interactions between eight billion people.

The *resistance* of the old Westphalian states is the inevitable, but dysfunctional, consequence of this. The rulers of such states defend the traditional culture as well as their professional interests, and are anchored in a perilous conservatism which risks leading to the negation of other systems of meaning. With this objective, they seize and manipulate, for better and for worse, the resources conferred on them by national and international institutions, established diplomatic-military practice, and codified international law. They mendaciously abuse traditional references to competition and power, even though these have demonstrated their ineffectiveness. They thus continue to instil the old hierarchical culture which results in contradictory results, exacerbating symbolic tensions and misunderstandings, and forever linking hegemony to arrogance and threat, thus resuscitating the old comforts of the struggle of 'good against evil' that disfigures the complex face of the world and dangerously confuses right with might.

The West suffers from this now as much as it did in the past,[11] and this paradoxically often makes every victory Pyrrhic. Thus, in the Ukrainian conflict, the defence of international law by the Western powers is obscured by an unexpected defeat suffered in the battle for meaning waged against the countries of the Global South who allow themselves to be convinced by Russian diplomacy of the persistence of a hegemonic spectre incarnated by a bellicose and somewhat entrenched West, cultivating the poisonous virtues of the 'one of us'.

The job of a specialist in international relations is definitely not easy. How can anyone forget that experts themselves have their own systems of meaning that distort their view? How, in these conditions, could they ever present themselves as neutral and above the semantic fray? How can they adhere to the naive virtue of exteriority which, according to Gary King, Robert Keohane and Sidney Verba, leading thinkers of American political science and authors of an authoritative manual, ban all personal experience of the researcher?[12] Perhaps what is needed, on the contrary, is personal involvement, committing oneself honestly and openly in a world that is never foreign to the observer[13] and displaying one's personal experience – an experience that allows one to go beyond the obvious and, sometimes, to lay bare problems, hypotheses and interpretive avenues to which dispassionate research could never have gained access without this intensified subjectivity.[14]

This interactive, interpretive sociology must therefore emancipate itself from the dead hand of an old-fashioned geopolitics that leads it towards illusion and error (chapter 1). It must look with a new eye at this diverse and plural international scene, without forgetting that this latter confusingly combines an unprecedented reality and a resilient institutional past that continues to haunt the dreams of those nostalgic for *realpolitik* (chapter 2). It must ask new questions about social actors, about their relationship to an otherness that is more decisive than ever, about the ever-changing context in which they act, and about the inevitably uncertain 'fusion of horizons' (chapter 3). It must finally reconsider the fragility of the new international relations. This fragility involves four major tensions that run like cracks through the contemporary international order: incomplete recognitions; the effects of differently perceived

Introduction

contexts; forms of diplomacy conceived in line with increasingly diversified codes; and, finally, a crisis of power that in various places is assuming particular and unexpected meanings (chapter 4). This sociology thus promotes what has become a necessary transfer, from a science of power towards a sociology whose aim is the most delicate of mutual understandings.

I
The Return of Geopolitics: A Nostalgic Illusion or a Recurrent Error?

All the time, in political or media rhetoric, at the militant opposite extreme from this intersubjective approach, people continue to use the term geopolitics: they speak of a 'geopolitics of Covid', of sport, or cinema, and so on. Recently, we have even seen a 'geopolitics of the Eiffel Tower', followed very closely by a geopolitics of Santa Claus! An American researcher, as if stunned by this sudden inflation, devoted an article to the subject to show, with supporting figures, that this surge began in Anglo-Saxon publishing in 2007 at the time of the financial crisis, hitting its stride in 2013, then lastingly awakening old uses that had almost disappeared since the Cold War.[1]

The semantic wind that is now blowing is doubly significant. It reveals a geographical obsession that has long gripped those responsible for thinking about international relations, but it testifies at the same time to the ostensibly neutral and objective desire to establish forever the force exerted by the structural determinants of international relations. According to this paradigm,

The Return of Geopolitics

human beings are dependent on the arrangement of the world, on the positions and locations imposed on them, further setting up territory as a currency of exchange through which the vanquished pay their debts to the victors. This current fashion also expresses a nostalgia: faced with the rise of a globalization that disturbs us and forces us to rethink everything, the geopolitics of our ancestors seems to have something reassuring and understandable about it, diluting in eternal maps all those principles and new forms of action that we fear because we do not know how to deal with them. Geopolitics claims to free us from the embarrassment caused by this tremendous growth in subjectivity and in the freedom to choose outside of determining factors.

But what lies behind this hackneyed term? The use is so common today that it turns out to be highly elastic. Sometimes a simple synonym for 'world politics', it then becomes all-purpose, a sort of generic term including any reflection on the world: it thus loses part of its conceptual force while becoming more ambiguous and relying ever more on implicit presuppositions. Sometimes overtly intended to introduce spatial parameters into understanding international relations, it then becomes as self-evident as it is annoyingly partial, since there are so many other components of the global game, combining freedom of action and decision, social dynamics, transnational forces of all kinds, and countless sectors of human action, certainly not limited to politics alone.

The contemporary avatars of geopolitics are most revealing: at the time of the Cold War, such an approach suggested that human beings depended solely on relationships of force and power, the 'balance of terror' between the East and the West which comprised the new law of history. But this approach was already challenged in its time – by the first failures of power in Vietnam and elsewhere, by the wave of decolonization, starting in the lower strata of societies, and especially by the first transnational beginnings of globalization. The recent revival of the concept has been promoted, at the same time, by autocratic dreams, those, among others, of Vladimir Putin and Recep Tayyip Erdoğan, who both saw in it a precious means of imperial restoration, and by those nostalgic for blocs and polarities, who found in it something to justify the sustainability of the old alignments – those alliances as durable as they were 'natural', of which NATO is one of the best contemporary illustrations. In reality, what is lurking here is the chilling spectre of a theory that took root at the end of the nineteenth century, only to meet a tragic fate. Its philosophy, somewhat loud and self-important at the time, but now discreet or even forgotten or hidden, is being shaken up by this complex world of intersubjectivity, while sometimes clinging on for quite a while in a tenacious nostalgia.

The foundational times of geopolitics

Let us return to the last quarter of the nineteenth century, when the map of the world's states was consolidated, indeed almost ossified, and set out to lastingly represent the future of the human race. A new vision emerged at the instigation of Friedrich Ratzel, the German geographer who came to his adopted discipline via pharmacy and the natural sciences. Influenced by Darwin, he saw in the rise of states the effect of a true law of evolution which, in its basis and even in its territorial essence, forever reconciled human beings with the laws of nature, bringing them under the yoke of their environment. Territory thus became a central issue, whereas previously it had been just one object of dispute among others. From this perspective, somewhat nuanced in Ratzel's work, stemmed all the simplifications that created the saga of militant geopolitics, notably the famous thesis of *Lebensraum*, that sufficient but necessary 'territory' for the life of a people who were inevitably led, by a sort of vital energy, to a drive for expansion.[2]

It is easy to see why this idea was popular among the conquerors, first and foremost Hitler, leading up to Putin today.[3] This resolute anti-humanism re-establishes the idea of a nature prior to the chain of determinants, dangerously opening up a slippery slope that would grow less threatening among the majority of more contemporary disciples but would always influence their plans, insofar as 'space matters more than ideas, and maps than chaps'.[4] It is an anti-humanism that trivializes war, updating an old Hobbesian reflex presenting states as eternal 'gladiators'. The German geographer Karl Haushofer fits comfortably into this tradition, as he views geopolitics as the 'science of political life as it is formed in living natural space'.[5] This is a very strange epistemological cocktail – one that has been at the heart of Western understanding of the world for quite a while.

Let us read Émile Durkheim's (measured) critique, in *L'Année sociologique* of 1899, of the *Anthropogéographie* that Ratzel had just published. In this study, Durkheim opened the way to a debate that would become central:

The Return of Geopolitics

It has still not been proven that this limited influence [of the soil on man] maintains the same intensity at different moments in history. It seems, in fact, that it tends more and more to weaken. ... Thanks to the greater ease of communications, the fashions, tastes and customs of different regions become more and more homogeneous. ... Indeed, as people increasingly associate the soil with their lives, transforming it for their use, it becomes, to the same extent, more difficult for them to separate from it. But here, if there is still a relationship of dependence, it is almost the opposite of that which we observe originally. If, this time, society clings to the soil, it is not because it has suffered its action but, on the contrary, because it has assimilated it. It is the soil that bears society's mark rather than society being modelled on the soil. It is therefore no longer the earth which explains man but man who explains the earth, and, if the geographical factor remains important for sociology to know, it is not because it sheds new light on sociology, it is because it can be understood only through sociology.[6]

Durkheim had thus already stated the essence of the matter at the end of the nineteenth century, contrasting sociology with geography.[7] He teaches us a valuable twofold lesson. On the one hand, he discreetly highlights the process of the social appropriation of territory, thus dealing a first blow to the geopolitical *doxa*: while territory was once merely a currency of exchange between princes, it has become, with modernity, a social good intimately linked to society, thus quietly announcing that wars of conquest would become increasingly difficult. This was the clearest possible intimation of the resilience of societies as revealed, over the following decades, by the processes of decolonization and the growing failure of external military interventions. On the other hand, Durkheim suggested all the implications of the socialization of territory and the transformations that resulted: territory is no longer a simple material good but is now part of the social dynamics resulting from globalization, especially in the tormented interplay of identity claims and of transnational relations and exchanges. Socialization and globalization are the two fundamental principles that are reshaping international relations.

Geopolitics tends to essentialize human beings as agents of a territorial patchworking. No margin is left to them either as individuals or even as aggregates in active social communities. The suffix 'political' then takes on its full meaning: in this vision, mediation between human beings and the soil belongs quite naturally to the state which, by the same token, becomes the only valid actor in international relations, the only one to be taken into consideration, the only one to be endowed with international credibility. This idea was also developed by a Swedish professor of political science, Rudolf Kjellén, who was deeply influenced by Ratzel and who popularized, in Gothenburg where he was a professor, the label of 'geopolitics'. The circle was now closed: what happened afterwards would perhaps be more measured, but would it never break with the cognitive pattern thus established. International relations lost their human essence and expressed the dynamic of a timeless and physical nature, forged by the map of the world, which incited a spirit of conquest that was destined to be the driving force of history.

Is geopolitics outdated?

Can we, in these conditions, conclude that geopolitics is now an outdated approach, valid only for its time, so that Émile Durkheim was the prophet of a new world? Could geopolitics simply be the outmoded projection of the desire for an absolute territoriality born from the failures and the tragic decomposition of Western feudal society? This hypothesis is tempting in more ways than one. Ratzel, Haushofer, Kjellén, Mackinder and many others were, despite the outrageous abuses to which their work fell prey, lucid witnesses of their time and especially of their history. Their geographical translation of the Westphalian order was probably not in the least exaggerated: territory was, in and after the Renaissance, an uncontested marker of power, and princes, backed by their plenipotentiaries, relied on it to sovereignly define and redefine the compromises ensuring their coexistence, in line with military vicissitudes and the hazards of war. This was the time of traditional interstate negotiations outside of any social process. The Congress of Vienna (1815) was its apotheosis, and even became the emblem which Henry Kissinger did not fail to brandish when he called for a settlement of the Ukrainian conflict by a rectification of the borders in the old-fashioned way, in complete ignorance of societies and peoples.[8]

This is a tradition into which Clausewitz, Carl Schmitt and Hans Morgenthau fit quite logically. Clausewitz demonstrates the perfect continuity between the military act and the political act, without the slightest social mediation, by logically insisting on the 'decisive battle' that inevitably reframes power and reconfigures the map of the world: here we clearly find the origin of the 'Grand Strategy' that would become dominant from the end of the nineteenth century; in it, princes articulate a national, clear and shared political objective, involving the consensual mobilization of appropriate resources.[9] Schmitt validated this princely vision of international relations, a vision that decrees enmity and *objectively* imposes it on an entire people to consolidate the nation to which this people is now subject, independent of any choice that could stem from a subjectivity more absent than ever.[10] And in 1948 Morgenthau translated this vision into a scientific theory, realism, which founded the science of international relations on a balance of power that geopolitics presents to us in the form of a map constantly being rectified according to circumstances and power relations.[11] These crucial figures, it seems, would tend to lead one to historicize the subjectivity that later slowly arose from the emancipatory process of societies, accelerated by the effect of globalization: imperceptibly but historically, there would be a shift from the objective order to the subjective order.

The explanation is obviously too simple, and the truth lies somewhere in the middle. No one would dare assert that the human being had suddenly gone from passivity to activism, from international relations as merely suffered to international relations as actively produced. On the other hand, there is no doubt that political practice has evolved and even transformed itself in this direction. From a monopolistic conduct of the international realm there stemmed a marginalization and even an exclusion of social actors, ensuring the ascendancy of geopolitics over thought. Thanks in particular to the spread of easier modes of communication already pointed out by

Durkheim, the irruption of societies broke this monopoly. The complexity of globalization has gradually introduced a diversity of sectors of social intervention, mixing politics, economics and culture without any of them being able to become dominant. Territories and geography found themselves swallowed up in this complex system: they did not disappear, of course, but lost control of the causal chain forever.

We will see later that the Vienna Congress nevertheless remains firmly anchored in the minds of most of today's political actors. We are familiar with the success still enjoyed by geopolitics among many observers who are keen to see the past return, as with dictators or simply 'old-fashioned' conquerors who find it difficult to imagine that the subjectivity of the rank and file could hinder the plans of professional gladiators. This naivety cost Vladimir Putin a resounding failure in his plans for conquest in Ukraine, just as it led to an impasse, even a fiasco, for the great powers that heedlessly intervened in Africa or the Middle East. More generally, few contemporary leaders agree to resort to new grammars of international relations that do not conform to their own.

This is where traditional geopolitics is reassuring: it still allows us to glimpse, in this complex world, a single, easy-to-grasp schema, especially when, following Halford Mackinder, it makes Eurasia the heartland of the world, abandoning the rest to the marginality characterizing the 'third world' of the past. This is how the Russo-Ukrainian conflict seems to have awakened everyone, giving the illusion that the war had 'recaptured' the essential, once again consigning the hotspots of Africa and the Middle East to the margins of near indifference. But they thereby forgot, unlike the old geopolitics, that this new conflict had reached unprecedented levels, establishing itself as the first 'globalized war' whose capacity for multi-sectoral and spatial expansion was limitless, and that a third party, around emerging countries and the Global South, threatened to be its final arbiter. Permanence and change intertwine, but the former seems to stifle the latter in the minds and decisions of princes.

Geographic renewal

It is obvious that this observation in no way signifies any overcoming of, or even crisis in, geography as a social science: on the contrary, the obsolescence of geopolitical paradigms makes the geographer crucial to the reinvention of knowledge that globalization demands in this context of growing intercommunication and partial deterritorialization. A more fluid space needs to be envisaged, more adapted to mobility and more interdependent on other spaces. This is the message of the pioneering work of Olivier Dollfus[12] and Jacques Lévy,[13] while, in Great Britain, Gearóid Ó Tuathail[14] is endeavouring to invert the conventional approach by showing how socio-political dynamics *reinvent* space, particularly under the effect of social pressures exerted on the margins, within populations that are poorly integrated into or ignored by the institutionalized order, thereby relativizing any balance of power. He concludes significantly: 'The term geopolitics is a convenient fiction, an imperfect name for a set of practices within the civil societies of the Great Powers that sought to explain the meaning of the new global conditions of space, power, and technology.'[15]

The Return of Geopolitics

Here, Ó Tuathail joins Durkheim in indicating that social appropriations permanently challenge territorial configurations by obeying other logics that are imbued by humanity, that is to say by mental reinterpretations of the imposed order, but that also involve frustrations, humiliations, expectations and social mobilizations. There are thus many elements that destabilize the simple logic of power and place subjectivity at the very centre of the enigma. And there are many parameters, many actors with fragmented and complex rationalities,[16] transforming the world into a thick web of multiple and intersecting meanings. Faced with this new configuration, the state – as praised in his time by Kjellén – no longer has the role it once played but is giving way to a proliferation of actors defying any centralizing pretensions and preventing yesterday's strategists from achieving their goals as they did in the past. The army itself is affected: it had been a tool of royal power when the state arose, but it is now coupled with countless private militias that were thought to have been dead for centuries, even affecting Putin's Russia, constantly struggling with the 'Wagner group' that was initially an auxiliary outfit but very quickly became an autonomous force and even a rival to states and their agents, or even a multinational mafia system incorporating economic, social and media dimensions.

But above all, in this race for extreme diversification, 'geopolitics' loses its initial epistemological pretension, the self-proclaimed value as a total paradigm that is still sometimes attributed to it. It retains merely a descriptive and partial virtue: it examines the conservative interplay of states and focuses on territorial issues, and thus nowadays expresses only part of the complexity of the global game and fails to explain most of the failures suffered by those who are too loyal to it. The world is no longer geopolitical, since geography is no longer, as Durkheim already asserted, just one global science among others – and also because the global is not exclusively political, and the state is no longer 'taboo', as Jacques Lévy puts it,[17] no longer embodying by itself all international rationalities. And, above all, it offers countless interstices where arbitrary decisions and unforeseen social dynamics can be expressed, where conflicts of meaning and misunderstandings develop, finally breaking down any deterministic relations. Hence the importance, at each of these stages, of reintroducing subjectivity, of considering individuals in the complexity of their rationalities, their culture, their emotions and their judgements; hence the need to revisit the international context to grasp the particularity of each history.

Once we have moved beyond geopolitics, does this latter basically remain the mere paradigm of an obsolete history specific to these centuries which separate the Renaissance from the bipolar world? It is true that these times lent themselves more to the *doxa* of geopolitics than today's globalization. But is this not ultimately the result of a historiographical illusion? Mutual understanding has never ceased to be a destructive issue for all structural certainties: before globalization, it was expressed in such a discreet atmosphere that it seemed – prematurely – to prove geopolitics right. Matteo Ricci and Michele Ruggieri announced, in their own way, the first breaches already opening up in this traditional approach when they sought to extend their Jesuit faith by compromising with the culture specific to sixteenth-century China, and thus set out in search of new understandings. Their brothers did the same in Latin America. But, by going too far in mutual understanding, they soon aroused the distrust of princes and of Rome, only to sink into the 'quarrel of rites' that put an end to their project in a highly instructive way.

In fact, these twists and turns in modern history had not deprived interstatism of its position as a well-crafted ideology. This vision remained the shared mode of description of international relations, hardly separable from the rituals of Europe. However, it never deeply affected the rest of the world and is no longer, today, an accurate representation of the complexity of the international scene – or, rather, it inspires outdated and failing practices that reveal how geopolitics is showing its age, neglecting or seriously underestimating the effects of intersubjectivity that are manifest in growing social mobilizations and the transnational fractures that result from them, in Ukraine and elsewhere, as during the Arab Spring, in Iran and in Africa. This new orientation stems first and foremost from the changes specific to the international scene that is increasingly spreading into new and multiple sectors of human activity, going far beyond traditional 'international politics'.

2
The Two International Scenes and Their Multiple Meanings

Beyond the uncertainties of geopolitics, there is still an international or, more precisely, *global* space, often dematerialized, more complex than in the past. 'Scene' or 'arena', 'international system' or 'society': some even go so far as to speak of 'international community', as if to provoke the proponents of a realist orthodoxy who, under the auspices of Thomas Hobbes, their master, see the international game as merely an endless rivalry between individualized sovereigns, stripped of any other incarnation. There is something vain in these quarrels: everyone knows that international life in no way corresponds to this deep and lasting affection by which we define the sociological concept of 'community'. However, no one can deny the recurrence and creative density of the interactions that take place between competitors or mere neighbours, whether they love or hate each other. This is what the social sciences consider more prosaically as a 'systemic effect'. However, in the race for objectivism, and amid all this art of reification, we have forgotten two essential facts: each actor in the same system does not see it in the same way; and societies, on the one hand, and princes, on the other, tend to foster an increasingly distinct vision of it. This is the twofold contemporary basis of many of the misunderstandings specific to our discipline.

As if to avoid such ambiguity, the proponents of the realistic *doxa* seek to deny or at least to neglect this very complex systemic reality: it is as if the gladiators no longer even had an arena! There is a curious paradox here: the proponents of objectivism dismantle the materiality of the international game while a subjective construction tends to give it new meaning. The truth probably lies somewhere in between: the system effect creates an objective reality that is simply understood and perceived *differently* by different actors. But there is another consequence: in reality, in this epistemological turbulence, *two* international scenes confront or overlap. One, dating back to Westphalian times, is defunct, although the princes believe they can keep it alive; the other is alive and more subtle, being linked to changes over the course of time and in particular to globalization, which organizes its activities. This enormous gap puts pressure on international politics on a daily basis. These many new projects are all being opened up by the subjectivist approach that we are examining.

A short subjective history of the international arena

Many misunderstandings stem from this: the modern international system, the one that still inspires diplomatic language and the international law that is supposed to govern us, was invented by Renaissance Europe as the logical and absolute outcome of the

Two International Scenes and Their Multiple Meanings

creation of the post-medieval nation-state. Admittedly, many interactive systems existed before, based around empires, ancient kingdoms, city states, and even various traditional segmental systems.[1] But rigour leads us to note that they were not 'international' in the strict sense of the term; they did not regulate the competition between sovereigns deemed equal. Above all, this system, of European origin, is the only one to have become universal, whether by force, trickery or routine. Officially, it still lives and reigns.

As a result, its deeply subjective nature has a twofold significance: the meaning it carries is external, sometimes even contradictory to that conceived by the extra-European world, and in particular that of the Global South; moreover, the meaning it had in the time of Hobbes, the Holy Roman Emperor Charles V or the French King François I obviously no longer corresponds to the contemporary data of globalization. And yet it remains, almost unscathed, in the principles it proclaims and the forms it displays, barely amended in terms of institutions and practices. But its meaning has been completely changed. Present issues are linked to this major contradiction, an inevitable source of intense destabilization. They now encourage us to '(re)provincialize Europe', to consider it as just one piece in the 'global jigsaw puzzle', as postcolonial thought suggests.[2] They can also lead us to update – even on the old continent – an outdated model, one still too imbued with the old Hobbesian gladiatorial ethos: these are the battles over meaning that are about to be fought.

In this case, this 'first system' is quite odd and almost contradictory, because it empirically conceived the international realm on the basis of a postulate that stifled it from the beginning: that of the sovereignty of each partner, a sovereignty that could not in the slightest be abdicated. In traditional theory, then, an international system exists only in the balance of opposites, of competing powers, or even of the 'terror' that organizes their relationships: its identity takes shape only in the coexistence between national interests that are endlessly locked in opposition. This is a complex and therefore fragile meaning, far removed from other systems of understanding, and it is a meaning based on a second paradox: the *international* system that the thinkers of the time, Hobbes and Grotius in particular, claimed to be universal was de facto reproduced, for centuries, as a *regional* and in fact exclusively European system, gradually and with difficulty extended to the American continent.

By adopting the Monroe Doctrine (in a message from the president to Congress on 2 December 1823), the United States first sought to distinguish itself from that system in the name of another system of meaning, at the same time more messianic and more particularistic. What was prematurely designated as 'isolationism' was part of a different reading of the world and now drew a contrast between European interstatism and the prophetic strains of the descendants of the *Mayflower*. But it was precisely this messianic aspiration which little by little encouraged the equivocal rallying of American power to the idea of a single, globalized system. But the initial 'regionality' of the international system – which did not yet speak its name, though it made no secret of universalist ambition – would gradually become the mother of all misunderstandings: European and American leaders took it for granted that their own vision should gradually extend to the whole world, while perceiving states – which were born outside their field – as belonging to a 'periphery', even a 'third world' that would need to develop and 'adapt' before playing a major role. This world region, now Euro-Atlantic, gradually became a closed club, convinced of its own ascendancy: this first took the form of the Concert of Europe, then the League of Nations, which, in the mind of Lloyd George, was its natural extension, then the United Nations, where the old powers imposed themselves as four of the five permanent members of the Security Council, and finally the G7, of which they had a monopoly, excluding the emerging powers. These latter seemed finally to appear in the G20, which became a group of heads of state in 2008 but quickly declined on the diplomatic radar.

This strategic confusion between the regional and the international realms lies behind a particularly remarkable battle for meaning which has shaped contemporary history. The clear entry of American power into the traditional international game took material shape in the Europeanization of the United States, notably through their active participation in the two world wars on the soil of the old continent and the construction of their hegemony through NATO, whose *raison d'être* was essentially European. This long process, timidly initiated when Washington sent a delegation to the Berlin conference on the Congo Basin (1885), had already been prepared by an adjustment of the meaning of the Monroe Doctrine, subtly amended by the terms of Manifest Destiny (1845). If American identity retained its originality, it was now explicitly thought of in a 'geopolitical' way, in the gradual elaboration of its imperial vision, based on a sense of divine mission and a claim to universalism, as President James Polk said at the time. This fusion of meaning is enlightening: now presenting himself as a conqueror determined to push the border of the confederation westwards and then to the Pacific, Polk opened the way for his successors who were quick to broaden the doctrine by looking southwards, and soon to the rest of the world. This extensive vision of conventional geopolitics did not escape the notice of the German geographer Friedrich Ratzel on his visit in 1873 to the United States, where, on his own admission, he found a sanctified variant of the theory of *Lebensraum*. This inaugurated the long career of the idea of the 'power projection', and from it stemmed an interminable conflict of understanding.[3]

Two shifts in meaning thus impacted on the international configuration for a long time: a shift from identity towards universality – they would prove to be reconcilable only by a hierarchical view of cultures, one that legitimized colonization; then, a shift from the region towards the world, gradually allowing the former to assume responsibility for the efficient management of the latter. Hence the recurring semantic confusion, particularly acute these days, between international cooperation and imitation, often translated as submission. We immediately note the institutional confirmation of these trends through the creation of a set of organizations aiming to be both regional and international, such as NATO or the OECD.

Playing on this confusion, NATO defined itself as both a regional pact and a global agent, witness its recent interventions in Libya, Afghanistan and Iraq and its desire to extend to a despatialized West so as to include Japan and Israel. This elasticity is fully realized in the fetish idea of 'special responsibility', frequently drawn on by Western powers to intervene in various parts of the world and to transcend the norm of the right of peoples to self-determination. The semantic battle reaches its climax when the dominated or marginalized states respond with the idea of 'solidarity', an idea officially meant to be disinterested but one that quickly assumed a formidable ambiguity.

Globalization has therefore imposed itself by following the most elaborate of contradictions, that which claims to universalize the particular ... This perilous mode has little by little given rise to a diplomacy of the Global South constantly torn between a cooperative norm and a tendency to protest: this creates the conditions for a profound renewal affecting the very nature of the direct or indirect conflicts between the old powers and the new states, for example in the exercise of the diplomatic function. The different sides do not have the same understanding of the situation: they are not seeking the same objectives. However, just by dint of functioning, the international system forms apparently common values and practices, seeming to build, over time, a 'society of states' linked by shared referents, as suggested by the English school of international relations.[4]

However, the father of this approach, Hedley Bull, has a sense of its ambiguities, which reside in more or less forced borrowings from dominant Western values, often challenged and at least inevitably reinterpreted by actors from other cultures:[5] the international system is in reality more 'cobbled together' (*bricolé*) than constructed, but this cobbling together (*bricolage*) has its share of reality, dictated by the argument of usefulness.

Two International Scenes and Their Multiple Meanings

As one can see, the existence of this 'society' is a question more than an affirmation: an infinite, unstable enigma, subject to the whims of circumstance and happenstance, a matter for research that requires us to re-examine, each time, the meaning of words and practices.

The semantic ambiguity of the international system: the perpetual conflict of meaning

In the absence of a strategist capable of grasping it, globalization has in turn been constructed as an aggregation of infinite choices, thereby leaving unanswered a question that has become essential, though hitherto ignored in practice: how are we to bring about convergence of such long and different histories; and how can political scientists – who themselves belong to a history – objectively conceive of the encounter with other paths to which they are foreign? Spontaneously, mainstream science followed in the footsteps of practitioners, approaching the relationships specific to a globalized world with a vocabulary that still came from Hobbes or Clausewitz. However, everyone enters this world with their own understanding but, above all, with the stigmata resulting from past and present clashes, all deriving from this perilous lack of understanding: in this matter, instead of drawing closer, meanings diverge more and more under the effect of increasing interactions. The Opium War remains emblematic in the collective consciousness of the Chinese, not only because it established a new domination and a lasting humiliation, with all the attendant suffering and destruction, but also and above all because it marked the sudden inanity of a code on which the Middle Kingdom has been based for more than three millennia. Hence the obsession of contemporary Chinese diplomacy to embark on a new battle for international norms in which China will no longer need to be 'subject' to those of others.

China, then, is no exception in this more or less explicit game: here we find the basis of the demand, so popular in the Global South, for the creation of a 'new world order', economic, political and legal. The idea was born at the Afro-Asian Bandung Conference (1955), and it gave substance to the Non-Aligned Movement that took over, leading in particular to the concept of development. This concept was itself mechanically torn between two opposed interpretations: the dominant one – a slow evolution guided by imitation of the Western model; and another, quite different one, formed in reaction to it, and aiming to achieve different trajectories that depended on histories and cultures. The science of international relations must therefore be (re)constructed, starting from a perspective of these visions of the world that were formed over the centuries, and indeed millennia, that preceded globalization. These visions do not disappear under the sudden pressure of the new parameters of the global order. On the contrary, they lead to increasingly divergent reinterpretations of globalization, to modes of entry into its meandering paths which remain dominated by acute conflicts of meaning that dictate the strategic choices of each party.

The *representation of the world* carried by each person is linked to the desire to position oneself in a favourable way while reconstructing the identity of the outsider. This is the starting point of the mechanical 'provincialization of Europe' that Chakrabarty speaks of. But this process is not merely cultural – far from it: it is historical, resulting from necessarily diversified experiences and opportunities. The Renaissance and the Enlightenment in Europe sought to overcome this difficulty by appealing to a Reason constructed by Western civilization but with an overtly universal scope – a Reason that could export and even forcibly impose its ideas and was in any case hierarchical in nature. Other ways of naming the world persist, however, and are even reawakening under the impact of global competition: it is high time to take them fully into account, no longer just to satisfy a taste for exoticism. They open up the conflict of meaning that marks our globalized world but at the same time lends itself to a complex game of strategic manipulation. It is this ambivalence that leaves its imprint on international relations.

In Chinese history, the Confucian tradition has for a long time drawn on the concept of *Tianxia* ('that which is under heaven'), a concept that, since 1990, has made a notable comeback.[6] The concept has the advantage of being the first designation of a universal, inclusive and global space, with a sense of globalization and its ascendancy in relation to the interstate competitive tradition that would intervene much later, being embodied by the *guo* ('state', one might say) that rests solely on strength. It can be argued that this ancient, valued tradition explains why China so quickly felt comfortable with globalization[7] and was able to take hold of it, give it meaning, and profitably develop its famous 'win–win' theory in international cooperative practice. It sheds light on the 'Silk Road' strategy that has significantly become the OBOR (One Belt, One Road) project. *Tianxia* thus provides a way of constructing a reservoir of meaning that shifts Chinese history away from the state norm of conventional borders and takes concrete shape in the multi-millennial idea of an empire with blurred margins.

At the same time, any system of meaning, this one as much as any other, does not in itself constitute a homogeneous political doctrine: a second epistemological sequence then opens up and describes the way in which an actor will manipulate this mode of understanding to their profit. Some argue, for example, that *Tianxia* can inspire and legitimize the reconstruction of the 'celestial empire',[8] others that it can promote the invention of a model of global governance,[9] while a third current suggests, on the contrary, that it leads to the reinvention of a 'conquering hegemony'.[10] So much freedom of choice is abandoned to each actor in power, thus validating the idea that nothing is written in advance. But, in all cases, *Tianxia* describes a mode of political production, makes it intelligible and gives it a meaning distinct from that which could obtain elsewhere, impacting all the more on the evolution of international relations. This also leaves us with two very sensitive questions for analysis: does this hegemony have the same meaning when its proponent does not have messianic aims and intends a general conversion? Do these shifts in meaning, even when reduced by the importation of nationalism from the West and the inclusion of the empire in the global game, explain the mysterious originality specific to foreign policies that remain essentially different in different parts of the world, hindering – irrespective of any ethical judgement – the 'fusion of horizons'?

The same cognitive tension is found with regard to Muslim worlds. The historical intimacy of the political and religious domains that developed here made the religious the natural emblem of all forms of political expression, both internal and external. In the modern era, the confusion in practice between globalization and domination has established religious symbols as almost the only instruments of affirmation and emancipation – instruments that were perceived, externally, as a constant source of threat, in particular by the *hegemon* who saw Islam as a dagger aimed at its power. Hence the complex reading of globalization in Muslim lands, where it is experienced both as a sequence that is the permanent basis for an absolute challenge to the traditional international order that emerged from the 'infidel world' and as a space of pragmatic accommodations with other states, understood as occasional and useful partners even when they did not belong to the same world. The reference to Islam serves as a basis for the expression of protest, while the useful contributions of globalization validate a subtle game of global integration: Saudi Arabia and, more generally, the states of the peninsula are, in this regard, exemplary. The Chinese conception of a naturally globalized world is thus opposed by the recurring vision of a fragmented, deliberately ambiguous global order subject to incessant battles.

The two systems: the system in theory and the system in practice

The past as thus constructed is difficult to erase, especially when it seems favourable to the decision-makers. However, globalization has disrupted the Westphalian situation in a way that is less rewarding for princes and,

Two International Scenes and Their Multiple Meanings

more generally, for politicians. This process has resulted, for example, in a gradual *social appropriation* of the international sphere, giving it a new meaning which no longer necessarily coincides with the Hobbesian meaning of yesteryear, even though this is the meaning that still underpins the cognitive schema of contemporary political actors. This results in a duality of systems: one is official, clearly visible amid the gilt décor of chancelleries, while the other is implicit, sometimes hidden in the twists and turns of society but often more decisive than the first. The irruption of society into the international game began timidly with the French Revolution, in which conscription, revolutionary messianism, the beginnings of social mobility, and the advent of various forms of irredentism played a major part. This development could have resulted in spectacular breaks, but nationalist ideology, largely controlled by the political order, contained what could have become an uncontrollable overflow of meanings: this new, popular formula kept social mobilization within the framework of an interstatism that even found itself reinforced through 'patriotism'. Hobbes was for a while reborn from his ashes.

Globalization has generated a completely different context. On the one hand, the spread of transnational relations has created new social solidarities, this time extended to the global level; on the international scene, it has intensified the pressure of non-political, economic, social and religious rationalities and has spread a globalized social imagination: the tensions between China and the West do not have the same meaning for traditional strategists as for American investors or the senior executives of Mercedes-Benz (one in two cars produced by this company is sold in China). On the other hand, this same globalization gives rise to new types of human behaviour everywhere, re-evaluating local identifications that forge and intensify new postures of protest.

The result of these changes is a distancing from traditional political institutions that are now less legitimate, less credible, and have sometimes even collapsed, together with a reinvestment in ethnic, family or religious allegiances and a rise in the strength of new social issues to which the therapies offered by states and nations are poorly adapted (climate change, food and health crises, gender and minority issues of all kinds, etc.). This results in new forms of mobilization and revolution which are gaining international relevance in their substance and their orientation (the Arab Spring, uprisings in Latin America in 2019, in Iran and in China in the autumn of 2022), but also and above all new modes of conflict, such as in the Sahel, the Congo, the Horn of Africa, Afghanistan and Yemen, in which power is no longer effective, states are severely challenged, and the rationalities employed are more social than politico-strategic. In short, the relationship with globality takes on a new meaning.

The gulf of misunderstanding that arises from this is gigantic. It sets a globalization that imposes itself by increasingly dominating the international agenda against governments that immediately retranslate this globalization into their own Hobbesian language. The conflict in the Sahel, which may be linked to social disintegration, is thus disguised as a sovereign war aimed at protecting France – or 'the West' – from the 'terrorist threat': this immediately leads to overlooking the incredible overlap of human and social insecurities,

Two International Scenes and Their Multiple Meanings

of institutional collapses, community rebirth, the privatization of violence and mafia flows. Thus, states can survive only by speaking their language, while the globalized scene is already using another. The Congresses of Vienna (1815) and Berlin (1885) are resurrected to settle the fate of Timbuktu or Tillabéri, as well as the tensions between Fulani and Dogons!

The real international system thus follows its own life outside the norms that supposedly regulate it, while decision-making actors still imagine themselves in a world which no longer exists, which they learned about at school or at university, and which had the advantage of giving them great value and even of belonging to them in their own right, as the idea of a 'regalian' domain suggests. At the same time, this duality, which is becoming commonplace, is in itself the basis for today's international game, becoming, as it were, its constitutive principle, the explanation for its failures, its aporias, the misunderstandings which become ritualized, the disappearance of victories and defeats, of imagined negotiations that never bear fruit. But we cannot neglect the fact that this huge contradiction revives, in its own way, the realistic theory which remains an indispensable dictionary that makes it possible to decipher the discourse of princes. The intersubjectivity that emerges in this atmosphere then reaches its optimum complexity: the two scenes face each other but barely understand each other, while each is being eaten away from the inside by increasing gaps in meaning.

3
Four Questions That Have Become Fundamental

In days when the present confusion concerning the very nature of the international sphere had not arisen, we approached this area with the same simple question, questioning power and the way it is implemented according to the strategic choices of each party in order to evaluate its performance: this was the absolute reign of power politics, the real credo of conventional geopolitics. As power gradually declined and demonstrated its growing inefficiency, it soon became necessary, after 1945, to add other parameters in order to understand the world: these would now naturally be discovered among the weaknesses or deviances of the adversary or simply of the new partners who were starting to proliferate: 'weak' or 'failed' states, and terrorism (the weapon of the less powerful), were singled out and gradually entered the new lexicons.

Have we really been able to progress by this new means? The new international scene, which is revealing, day after day, its subjective charge, is leading us

Four Questions That Have Become Fundamental

towards other paths and new questions which are now unavoidable:

1) How can we *identify actors* with international relevance, beyond traditional objective criteria?
2) How can we grasp the *meaning* of their initiatives, whether they are taken by decision-makers, with their very different cultural overtones, or by those actors, the simple pedestrians of globalization, who come from backgrounds that are sometimes very far from our usual codes?
3) How do they, each in their role, perceive a *context* that globalization has nevertheless made, for the first time, apparently unique and common?
4) How can we define, in these conditions, the *fusion of horizons* which seems to be the sine qua non for modern peace?

The identity of the actor is no longer a simple question

The international actor today is no longer the single omnipotent prince who 'mobilized', in all senses of the term, soldiers or plenipotentiaries in order to optimize his own interests, those of the kingdom, little by little transfigured into the postulated interests of the nation. We have gone beyond the absolute social passivity that sharpened Voltaire's irony, as he noted this game of tin soldiers, suffering their fate where 'the muskets swept away from this best of worlds nine or ten thousand ruffians who infested its surface.'[1] This is a world where everyone thinks internationally, beyond the role that was previously assigned to them; a world that potentially has as many actors of this nature as inhabitants – at least those of them who have acquired through age and experience a minimal awareness of the international sphere; a world whose stability depends in part on the degree of engagement of each person in the most diverse international acts that are no longer the monopoly of states or even of structured organizations.

Two subjectivities come together at the same time, in a complex and indecisive way, impacting more than ever on the rules of the method: the subjectivity of the *observer* and that of the observed *actor*. The involvement of the first in the international game can be strong or weak, conscious or unconscious, distanced or militant, but it is always present and determining. Even more so perhaps, if it is not made explicit. The analyst's posture entails a double subjectivity that must be controlled: that of perception and that of interpretation. The former describes (others would say 'constructs') the global space observed, whether total or partial, listing its actors and circumscribing its issues and depicting its context. The latter completes the analysis by giving meaning to the observed game and the rationalities that confront each other in it. In either case, the experience of observers is not neutral: each milestone in their life and their learning obviously guides their steps. If we are to understand the work of Thomas Hobbes (1588–1679), it is not irrelevant to remember that his personal life was punctuated by fears and insecurities: those inherited from a mother terrified by the threat of her homeland being invaded by the Invincible Armada that caused her to give birth prematurely; those attributable to a father who abandoned him at the earliest age; those deriving from the bloody Thirty Years' War that accompanied

Four Questions That Have Become Fundamental

his youth and later years; and those of the English Civil War that tormented him.

This pressure, coming from the sometimes intimate life of the analyst, throws things out of shape when it is not conscious, but it shapes them positively when it is rigorously put to use. Such was the richness of the American anthropologist Clifford Geertz, able to immerse himself in the depths of Javanese society in order to understand it and carry out the *Modjokuto* project dedicated to Javanese society which, in the 1950s, seemed called upon to play a central role in the post-war world order. This led him to live for many months in a family of local railway workers, inhabited by the 'pervasive nervousness' that accompanies the detection of differences in meaning and the questioning of the canonical self-evident 'facts' that derive from it.[2] Helped by knowledge of the field, and especially of the language, this somewhat feverish quest is probably the spur to a high level of productivity that no one can do without. Sparked by the complex identity of the researcher or by the circumstances in which he or she learns their trade, it is the source of all international research: based on ego-history or acquired experience, this contribution of the subjectivity of the observer is an essential asset when it is controlled, just as it makes the work invalid when it is absent, ignored or left aside.

Descriptive work becomes a crucial starting point, if only by drawing up the list of players and issues that, in international relations today, are not given in advance. Whether they are themselves actors or mere analysts, or even both, observers reinvent the international scene by imposing their own choices, in particular that of conceiving the true dimensions of the scene they are exploring. Thus, one analyst will take the risk of describing the Sahelian conflict as the action carried out by 'the French army against jihadist terrorists', thereby obscuring an impressive number of other actors with other issues: secessionist armies, such as the Tuareg groups, private and self-defence militias, warlords, mafia and criminal networks, but also village chiefs prey to famine and the throes of institutional disorder, not to mention a number of individuals, breeders or farmers, who are seeking land and fodder.

These are all constitutive agents of the new forms of conflict, ignorance of which becomes a major source of failure. This is obviously echoed by the complex subjectivity of each of the actors involved who, unlike in the past, do not see or conceive of the conflict in the same way, rejecting any common code, making negotiation all the more difficult to conceive. In the classical era, this consisted of a transaction that obeyed the rationality common to all interstate wars; today, we see a mixture of social, cultural and individual rationalities based precisely on the difference in positioning but also in language. Yesterday, the fiction of a national interest, wrongly imagined to be simple and obvious, imposed itself as a *doxa* common to almost everyone, setting the agendas of international relations. Nowadays, this fiction is no longer credible: the so-called national interest has become eminently subjective, the result of the only way in which each person thinks or interprets it, according to their convictions, their priorities and their wagers.

The imbroglio of modern conflicts is therefore obvious: with whom is it possible to negotiate, and who should we refuse to allow to come to our table? How can we include mafia leaders in a negotiation on which

Four Questions That Have Become Fundamental

the end of conflicts partly depends? Or a village chief whose space of perception is infinitely narrower? Or a warlord who has no interest in a peace that would deprive him of his main resource? And states from elsewhere, which are no longer, as in Westphalian times, driven by the competitive game of power but, pell-mell, by their desire to remain the suzerain power – the power to be recognized, to preserve their predatory ability and to benefit from the dividends of vassalage?

How are these conflicts of a new era to be managed, when intelligence itself is partially outside state control and is sometimes even in the hands of a private entrepreneur such as Elon Musk, in Ukraine, who decides and acts in line with a rationality all of his own. Globalization does its job perfectly well by giving rise to these many complex games, even within the old world: beyond the patina that makes a war of conquest obsolete, the Russo-Ukrainian conflict has generated the same countless behaviours of diverse and varied actors, overflowing state boundaries and coming to life even to the most distant horizons. There are economic, religious, media and sporting actors, but also and above all individual actors, close or distant, fearing starvation or wondering, each in their own way, what being deprived of energy might cost them. Everyone then looks at the foundations and solidity of the 'social resilience' familiar in Ukraine of course, but also spreading throughout Europe and beyond, becoming a composite and unprecedented unknown in the very evolution of the conflict.

Such an inflation of subjectivities undermines old fixed notions and ancient structures; it disrupts conventional paradigms and places the analyst in uncomfortable situations. It creates a new chapter in international relations by evoking the imbroglio described at the end of the Cold War by the American philosopher Richard Rorty, already aware of this complexity of human subjectivity. Suggestively, he referred to the 'hermeneutic circle' that now made it necessary to know the whole in order to understand the parts, but also to know each of the parts in order to understand the whole.[3] The thesis applies perfectly to the new global game, when nothing and no one is any longer the sole master of the game: individuals have never been, and structures are no longer masters, while princes were almost masters but can no longer claim to be; the quest for competing subjectivities and the surveillance of that of the observer are now the basis for the new method of investigation.

Acts and actors depend intimately on all the others, but that is where the difficulty lies: the circle is not closed, with each actor having his or her own rationality which is not necessarily always thought of in terms of international consequences. As for that mysterious totality, it is neither reifiable nor embodied, it cannot be controlled by anyone: the strategist is therefore in danger, hindered, limited, 'entangled';[4] only the resulting combination is king, but it is not under the control of any authority. Foreign policy is nothing more than a subtle mixture of soft reactivity and crazy imprudence.

Analysts themselves are fatally trapped in this same inflation of meanings. To use the terms of the German philosopher Wilhelm Dilthey, they become more and more dependent on the interaction between their personal experience and the understanding of the world that they derive from it, an understanding that is too complex to be objectified and to follow traditional typologies. We thus see the development, in contemporary thinking about international relations, of a 'psychologization of the transcendental', the exact opposite of the obsessive positivism of international and 'geopolitical' studies of yesteryear. This tendency favours, in Dilthey's own words, the blossoming of this 'first germ of the self and the world' that follows the discovery of the difference between one self and another.[5] One can sense its irreplaceable and necessary strength, but also its weakness and the risks it entails.

Thinking about the 'Other'

In this increasingly complex and expanded interactive game, the figure attributed to the Other obviously becomes a central piece of the international chessboard. To conceive of it, it is a matter of anticipating the behaviour and choices of my partners – something that has been true throughout all times – but also of deciphering their cultural universes and those of their fellow citizens, of determining what they accept and what they reject of the international order as it is, as well as the perception they have of myself and my own universe. The Westphalian schema had too quickly reduced every fighter to the figure of the Hobbesian gladiator, an incessant rival but similar to oneself, a sort of perennial double that interest leads episodically to mutate into a more or less durable enemy. The realist vision sticks to this and was definitively formulated by the American political scientist Quincy Wright, a pioneer in his field who stated that war involved the struggle of *people similar to oneself*.[6] The analysis of globalization must now lead beyond, to the discovery of this sociological diversity that gives rise to a plurality of rationalities, a variety of identities, each of which bears its own culture, and the knowledge of which, furthermore, is made difficult by the hazards of translation.

But there is something even more complex: the identity thus given to my adversary or my simple counterpart is, in a globalized world, the direct fruit of what my socialization has taught me. Ever since the work of the Austrian-American sociologist Peter Berger, we have known that the society specific to each actor imprudently defines what the Other is and thus collects official portraits, devastating caricatures that foster incredible prejudices.[7] Each story remakes that of the others in its own way, mixing affect, ignorance, prejudices and sincere errors of appreciation, easily sliding towards a form of negation of one's counterpart, and therefore to a dangerous underestimation of his or her capacities. Winston Churchill – who nevertheless knew what resistance meant – failed to grasp the decisive moment of Indian independence through a sort of strange negationism: 'Overall, Indians do not constitute a historic nation. Who hasn't conquered them? . . . Throughout their history, Indians have rarely enjoyed true independence.'[8] Gandhi was merely perceived as a 'half-naked fakir' who 'gave him chills', and Nehru – who had a more marked Western socialization, in his view – was only a 'high caste Brahmin' . . .

Decades later, and also in connection with a former colonial possession, did not President Macron wonder, on 30 September 2021, about 'the existence of an Algerian nation before colonization'? This reinterpretation of the Other from the Self's standpoint is a familiar reflex, especially among those who dominate, or at least who think they do; it has precisely the weakness of constructing the alternative identity based on its own criteria and its own representation of the world. The nation, an essentially Western concept, seems to imagine that the same 'geopolitical configuration' exists everywhere, the same texture of territories and borders, the absence of which would be equivalent to nothingness and the negation of any other form of political community. Thus, we impose on others weaknesses that we do not recognize in ourselves (have the old nations, for example, never been subject to conquest?). These dissonances become major facts in the history of international relations, which we marginalize by failing to see them appear clearly in the usual repertoire: Churchillian contempt played a certain role in the Germanophile impulses of Indian nationalists during the Second World War, then in the pro-Soviet sympathies of the Congress Party after independence, notwithstanding the efforts of Clement Attlee, while the condescending view taken in France of Algeria also pushed the latter to look for a long time towards Moscow.

Globalization thus gives a twofold complexity to the construction of otherness. On the one hand, this development must face cultural and historical gaps considerably wider than in the past: the shared code which was naturally imposed in Westphalian times and which was empirically constructed during the Cold War has had no real substitute since then, and the common socialization that international institutions could carry out remains too limited.[9] On the other hand, we must not fall into essentialism: cultural barriers are not walls of fire or concrete. So it is essential to take the construction of the Other's identity as a priority field of research, stripped of the culturalist presuppositions often linked

Four Questions That Have Become Fundamental

to geopolitics. A study of Sino-American relations shows this very clearly:[10] it reveals that nothing is definitive, that individual perceptions are not necessarily simply modelled on collective constructions, leaving a significant part of the destiny of international relations in the partially autonomous hands of the individual. The study in question indicates that the element of political and governmental manipulation is not negligible in the management of intergenerational cultures, suggesting that these are not fixed and that the horizons can draw closer. Finally, it shows the critical link between perception and trust, trust and cooperation. These are all avenues that give this question a much more decisive importance than the attachment to old structural factors would suggest.

Thus appears the core of a new sociological and comprehensive approach to international relations, leading to several essential questions: How can I understand the Other beyond my prejudices? How can I approach my own codes of international understanding? How does the Other himself or herself understand my own construction of the international sphere? How does he or she combine, in his or her decision-making, a choice of a subjective nature with the use of materials drawn from a transcultural rationality, as suggested by the stimulating analysis of 'poliheuristics' carried out by Alex Mintz, studying the choices made by the princes who govern, subtly mixing local and universal references?[11] What particular reading does the Other have of the international context which is apparently common to us?

These menacing discrepancies in meaning that lie in wait for us are due not only to the nation to which an analyst belongs but also to the weight that ideologies

Four Questions That Have Become Fundamental

exert on him or her, to the burning and increasingly intense temptation to sink into the ideologization of the world, relapsing into a deliberately schematic view that pits good against evil, the 'reason' that one knows how to cultivate against the 'fanaticism' of the other, democracy against dictatorships, as if it were that simple. Subjectivity thus has its pitfalls when it is neglected and not controlled by the rules of method, when it is the prisoner of beliefs or prejudices, emotions, or even hatred. Subjectivity is there for the best and the most essential, but also for the worst, which transforms it into a machine for demonizing or despising the other. As Dilthey noted, this psychologization of the transcendental must therefore lead, on this road, to 'cognitive empathy', the art of transposing oneself into the other in order to understand their thought patterns, the foundations of their own visions, instead of seeking to share their emotions, as is too often the case.[12]

The construction of the context

By this stage of the analysis, everyone agrees that context is a key element of the international game, even 'closing the loop' of the analysis by describing the set of circumstances allegedly *shared* by the actors who face the same issue.[13] However, the definition and understanding of context remain very delicate, even enigmatic: beyond the shared context presumed by the observer, is this 'sharing' real, assumed in the same way in different parts of the world? The weakness of the traditional analysis is to have excessively objectified the idea of a single and common international context, as if it were imposed on the actors in an identical manner, manufactured *ex nihilo* by divine providence or by a surface froth of history over which no one has any control and which everyone apprehends in the same way. This methodological fatalism is disastrous, as it relegates the human being to the rank of passive epiphenomenon, sealing destinies like a 'Thucydides trap', renewing forever the structural and belligerent rivalry between rising powers (as with China at present) and falling powers (the United States).[14] The disaster is two-fold: fate is ineluctable and history is uniform.

Constructivism has not really solved the problem: it is obviously too easy to assert that the context is simply manufactured by the actor.[15] Are industrialization yesterday and globalization today merely the effects of decrees that could easily be repealed, simply deciding to go for 'deindustrialization' or 'deglobalization'? The overlapping logics of *choices* and *constraints* lie at the centre of the international game, as this is made up of parameters which do not belong to the same temporality or rest on the same genetic mechanisms, much less the same processes of understanding.

The two examples we have given demonstrate that, beyond the mysterious structural effects and the choices of individuals, technology and its progress have a decisive impact, allowing actors not to *abolish* them but only to *adapt* them. Globalization could be abandoned only at the impossible cost of purely and simply eliminating modern communication techniques, but on the other hand it leaves an enormous margin in its *interpretations*, in the definition of its modalities (of which neoliberalism is only one variant) and of its purposes (the juxtaposed management of national interests or the integrated management of global assets, for example).

Four Questions That Have Become Fundamental

Moreover, it was this somewhat candid obsession with uniform globalization that had led Western princes to persuade themselves too easily that China's entry into the globalized economy would make it a liberal democracy similar to those current in Europe or North America.

The reality is elsewhere, and the method needs therefore to be revised: context is neither entirely created nor totally constraining, while this constraint is not understood or received everywhere in the same way. History is there to tell us where the context that we need to reckon with comes from and to help us distinguish what is fixed and what can be adapted within it, the 'clock' and the 'cloud'.[16] But the political science of international relations should also allow us to approach three highly sensitive sequences at this stage of the analysis: How does each actor *conceive* the context in which he or she acts? How do these inevitable *conflicts of meaning* and interpretations that derive from them in turn become major parameters of the international system at a given moment in time? How does such a game of uncertain mutual understanding then modify the *behaviour of the competing actors*?

Colonization, decolonization and postcolonization are in themselves three examples illustrating the approach. For formerly dominated countries, decolonization is experienced not as a simple episode in their history but as a lasting and new representation of the world that strongly influences the interpretation that their populations give of it. This unprecedented understanding reflects on the way the more general context of the Cold War is read: we have already seen that it had in its time given rise to the Afro-Asian conference

Four Questions That Have Become Fundamental

in Bandung, and to non-alignment; it has little by little dramatically underlined the features of otherness and made external intervention unbearable; it has given everything that makes it possible to differentiate oneself from others – religion, symbols of identity, normative expression – a determining and often invasive force, sometimes aggressive or intolerant.

In accordance with the proposed reading grid, these dissonances create different representations of a context produced by the very same events. Thus, the link to colonial history reconstructs, in the 'Global South', the context specific to the Russo-Ukrainian conflict, giving rise to a Western incomprehension of Afro-Asian abstentions in the UN General Assembly votes intended to sanction Russia. While the West viewed the circumstances as jeopardizing the territorial integrity of a European state, in the South it was simply a question of a conflict between Northern powers, endangering the human security of the poorest populations and maintaining 'double standards' at a time when no one was concerned about the de facto annexation by Israel of the Palestinian territories that seemed closer to those populations. Western diplomacies experienced the greatest difficulty in adapting to this unprecedented reading of the context as it was perceived outside their sphere of belonging, while Russian diplomacy saw it as an advantageous way of quickly developing bilateral relations that could not fail to seriously disorient the followers of geopolitics: collusion with Turkey, a NATO member; with Saudi Arabia, a faithful heir to the Quincy pact which formerly linked it to the United States; and even with Pakistan, the United Arab Emirates, Israel, or a number of African States. This multiplication of 'free diplomatic unions' has, in turn, created a new context unfavourable to the sustainability of old alliances. The context is not given: it is indeed constantly interpreted, even imagined, and therefore reshaped by the actors involved in line with numerous variables and vicissitudes.

What fusion of horizons?

In one way or another, these questions bring us to the common basis of all sociology: there is no social game without a minimal understanding between actors, without the *beginnings* of a fusion of meanings. International relations cannot be an exception. Even more: this minimum is, in this area, more vital than elsewhere, since it conditions war and peace, and, in the present atmosphere, this directly involves the survival of humanity. Like any paradox, this one is only apparent: Westphalian history preferred the relationship of power to the relationship of understanding, power to intersociality, so as to make princes and their policies the pivots of the world order. In an exclusively European world, the fusion of horizons once depended on a board game whose rules were de facto shared: there was nothing enigmatic about it, and it was based solely on gradients of force and cunning. In a globalized system, the reality is completely different: fusion is in itself a permanent and potentially belligerent enigma, whose ways people neither know nor wish to know, apart from the ways inherited from a bygone world. The question is therefore central to the agenda of princes and diplomats, as well as that of researchers and observers.

Yesterday's analysts hardly cared about this: it was enough for them to follow the dotted lines of geopolitics or the straight lines of rational choice and of the postulated and proclaimed 'national interest'. The analysts of today must make substantial detours: beyond territorial determinants, calculations of reason, vested interests, and the meanders of cunning, they must now question the compatibility of meanings at the same time as the real desire of actors to make this fusion possible. Humiliation, a traditional figure in contemporary international relations, is very revealing from this point of view. It is very often born from a misunderstanding whose path it is important to retrace: the meaning that Russian leaders give to their history, the history of both an empire and a nation-state, both European and Asian, Christian and yet drawing on the idea of a 'third Rome', is a perpetual source of incomprehension and humiliation, of revenge and assertiveness.

However, an analysis which is aware of these dissonances to the point of claiming to overcome them would come up against two joint cynicisms: that of the prince afraid of losing the advantages which he derives from the humiliations which he stages and that allow him to mobilize his people at little cost; and that of the victim himself who can advantageously monetize his humiliated status to the point of winning the support of those who, elsewhere in the world, perceive themselves as his companions in misery. Lack of understanding bears specific fruit: its sustainability, sincere or calculated, makes any peace solution, or even any real negotiation, more difficult; we will see that this is probably the cause of the gradual disappearance of any real international negotiation. Even more profoundly, humiliation creates a politically unmanageable meaning, as it arouses, among those who are its victims, both fascination and

Four Questions That Have Become Fundamental

detestation or, as Nirad Chaudhuri noted with regard to Indians, a behaviour which leads them to 'crawl' as well as to 'hate',[17] both to borrow and to distinguish themselves, and to sink into an absolute fluidity of relationships making any construction unstable. It then becomes difficult to really merge similar horizons!

Such a fusion therefore jointly imposes a deep understanding of the Other, an engineering of meaning, making the relationship between actors transitive. It is again connected to the 'cognitive empathy' of which Dilthey speaks, and which Geertz suggests may well come up against the non-translatable nature of certain modes of thought: *'tradutore, tradittore'*. Fundamentally, the 'fusional' project remains at the stage of understanding and cannot go as far as any sharing of emotions. The method is then that of the anthropologist, whose knowledge is too often absent from international analysis, and what is at stake is a humanism based on the conviction that the human dimension opens a way out of the impasse in two ways: by the desire for harmony or by access to the 'thought of thought' (*noêsis noêseôs*), in Aristotle's formula. The first of these paths evokes, through its utilitarianism, the way in which economic exchange contributes to stability in East Asia – via the element of peace that the antagonism between nations and cultures had seemed to make impossible. The second way, in the thought of Aristotle, was essentially divine in nature: but, all blasphemy against the Master aside, is this so true and so definitive? Is it not simply linked to the understanding of fundamental needs resolutely common to all of humanity, whether material (food, taking care of oneself, living in harmony with nature, etc.) or symbolic (recognition, dignity, respect)?

Four Questions That Have Become Fundamental

The fusion of horizons will in this case be impossible as long as we occupy a position in the mere opposition between subjectivities, in suspiciousness, and in the conspiracy mania that fuels many transnational networks: it will emerge only through the rediscovery of the primary needs that reconcile all thoughts. This is what David Mitrany suggested very early on, paving a way to the new imperative of global governance, a pragmatic and very often forced imperative, as stated and promoted later by Kofi Annan. But is such respect compatible with the manufacturing and sustainability of national interests (or so-called national interests), or even with nationalisms that play on them, or permanent stigmatizations?[18]

4
Rethinking the International Agenda

This intersubjective approach, as we have just defined it, makes it possible to uncover a certain number of ways – both cultural and strategic – in which the international agenda and the scientific agenda itself are dogged by concealed factors. In so doing, it makes it possible to identify the real issues linked to this lack of understanding, thus revealing other urgent issues than those commonly mentioned, issues that affect the stability of the international system in a much more serious way. Four sources of tension have emerged and influence the contemporary international order. These tensions stem from: first, a lack of recognition of the Other; second, an overly contrasting reading of the international context; third, the very use of the diplomatic instrument and the meaning given to it by both sides; and, finally, the diversified understanding of power, that old key concept of the discipline that no one dares to challenge but that everyone reshapes in their own way, spreading the greatest disorder everywhere.

The unavoidable battle for recognition

We are immediately faced with a paradox: recognition was quickly considered to be a centrepiece of the Westphalian game, but it was never treated as a fundamental problem. The gladiators of yesteryear had first to know and respect each other: recognition of the Other has always, for this reason, lain at the centre of the diplomatic institution. But it was still a *formal* recognition, designed according to criteria taken from old Westphalian practices. The act in question was essentially legal, leaving little room for the subjective dimension. Normative in essence, it left aside, right from the start, three associated subjective virtues, real guarantees of peace, the true foundations of full recognition: respect, esteem and trust.[1] This negligence was sometimes politically useful and still remains so: it provided flexibility in strategies and made it possible to embrace a dictator when necessary. On the other hand, it mechanically gives rise to increasingly dangerous shocks that constantly shake the international system: the eviction of respect fuels humiliation, the eviction of esteem frustration, and the eviction of trust duplicity. Hence the many highly subjective international pathologies that are common today but rarely analysed and even less discussed, and on which further work is necessary.

The first of these evils is illustrated by the aforementioned Opium War, and above all by the way that Chinese society has remembered it. At its origin, in 1839, Great Britain wanted to forcibly sell the Chinese Empire a product, opium, that it was forbidden to sell to its fellow Europeans: the difference in perception between Chinese who could be forced to consume deadly drugs and Westerners to whom it was inappropriate to offer them became a source of lasting dissonance and humiliation. The second evil is encapsulated in many images, but one exemplary case was the Western policy carried out in the nineteenth century towards the Ottoman Empire, during the time of the *Tanzimat*, the reforms imposed by the great European powers on a despised local power that was deemed 'sick', incapable and clearly inferior: we know what happened to Turkish–Western relations, and the incomprehension and suspicion that still linger today. The third, for its part, includes many diplomatic postures, in particular the mistrust in Sino-West relations, ever since Beijing was suspected of taking the upper hand in the management of globalization, and the relations between the West and a Muslim world perpetually viewed as a place of suspicion and devious plots. These three vices have a common root: the Other no longer exists except through the often negative image we have of it and the strategic manipulations we make of it. The need for recognition thus fades away in the face of the objective considerations of the moment. As a result, the relationship becomes permanently unstable, uncertain and conflictual.

This opens up a whole new field of research, albeit one little practised by those interested in international relations. In it, we also find the essential basis for defining any action that would be effective within the contemporary global space. Full and *equal* knowledge of this *social imaginary*, specific to the actors addressed, has become a necessary step, an unavoidable prerequisite for the production of any innovative foreign policy. This detour, now necessary in the imagination of others, relates to the 'quest for meaningful relationships' or even to the curiosity that encourages us to 'go and meet the unknown', in the words of Georges Balandier.[2] It becomes possible when we go beyond official discourses to immerse ourselves in anthropological observation, in the study of the literature of the countries concerned, in artistic and media production. Above all, it is important to take into account influencers, local political actors, religious figures, media and intellectuals.

Such an investigation makes it possible to effectively question the conditions for receiving a message sent by the author of a foreign policy or by any actor in a globalized policy. This imaginary of the Other – not limited to those in power alone – controls the interactive process that is created, decides its success or failure, and the modes of mutual understanding that are deployed. It creates the social expectations of the opposite party, as well as the latter's evaluation of its partners' initiatives: its careful analysis usefully shifts foreign policy from the strategic sphere to the behavioural sphere and allows us to understand how the Other is really understood within the global space. For example, Operation Barkhane,[3] considered rational in strategic terms, inevitably seemed untenable in terms of the scale of recognition of the societies concerned, the diversity of their components and their competing rationalities, the developing social expectations, and the perceptions they fostered with regard to potential participants, as well as the memories that were lost and found, and above all the issues experienced on a daily basis in each village: a microsociology of this kind has become an essential parameter of any international action undertaken. The same is true of American interventions in Iraq, Afghanistan or Somalia (1993).

Rethinking the International Agenda

From this point of view, the confidence naively placed in the mediation of soft power is misleading, as is the effect of the diplomacies of influence generally associated with it.[4] Soft power has a real effect of seduction: it certainly creates consumerist expectations among those who are exposed to it, but it does not necessarily gather support for the foreign policy of those who wield such power; contrary to popular belief, it does not correct this lack of recognition, as the more powerful party might have hoped. There is almost no transitivity between the consumption of intellectual or symbolic messages and adherence to the underlying political order. As for the diplomacies of influence, they deploy policies of persuasion that are generally counterproductive when the receivers feel humiliated or undervalued. The image of the transmitter is ultimately more decisive than the content of the message: this explains much of the disillusion currently created by postcolonial practices. We have already seen that the 'fascination–hatred' pairing combined the attraction aroused by the capacity of the dominant party and the resentment provoked by this inequality: it is more than ever constitutive of the scale of non-recognition that structures the international game.

These are all failures that lead directly to a *resentment* which, through its violent and belligerent effects, increasingly conditions the entire international system, as it does any social system. This reaction is actually expanding dramatically, as the German philosopher and sociologist Max Scheler argued: he is a very useful figure in this subjective reorientation of research. As a disciple of Dilthey and a follower of the phenomenological movement, he started from the idea that *lived* experience – which is perpetually reshaping memory – plays an essential role in knowledge, as to be expected in someone who was torn in his youth between the Judaism of his mother and the Catholic education he received at school. He logically presented resentment as a 'self-poisoning', frequent whenever a formally proclaimed equality is thwarted by the perceived rise in objective inequalities.[5] But globalization ticks all the boxes here, as it fosters the growing visibility of difference, helplessness and exasperation in the face of inequalities of various kinds.

However, resentment – which continues to take on a social dimension – remains a neglected, marginal, sometimes merely anecdotal parameter in international studies, even though it adds a new spin to the idea of recognition, opening a field of research into the subjectivity of the actor and the systemic effects that result from it. In particular, it leads the resentful person to manipulate symbols, to create meaning aggressively. Take the Polish writer Michał Czajkowski, who, in the nineteenth century, converted to Islam, became Mehmet Sadiq Pasha and joined the Ottoman army to mark his hostility to Russia, which had divided his country. He thereby inaugurated the modern history of militant conversions, such as we have seen proliferate since, notably during the Syrian conflict. Such conversions, among those who resort to them, are a critique of the lack of recognition from which they had to suffer at home. These 'converts' react by espousing an imaginary of global relevance allowing them to stigmatize and combat the failure of their societies on a broader level. The same applies to those today who, in another mode, brandish Russian flags in the streets of Bangui or Bamako in the name of a fantasized freedom, thus helping to create new diplomatic alignments ... The battle for meaning is partly crystallized in the twists and turns of this new imaginary: it tends to become an epicentre of new international relations without anyone really knowing how to study it or, even less, to remedy it, except through invectives and clumsy reactions that just make it worse.

This new kind of analysis leads to a *philosophical anthropology* of which the study of international relations should make greater use. Initiated by Scheler, this approach was extended by Helmuth Plessner, who sees human beings as distinguished by this endless negotiation between their physical nature and the contradictory and evolving conditions of their multiple socializations.[6] The author ends up deducing that there is an intrinsic 'unfathomability' to the actors involved, linked to the groping definition of their being in the face of an increasingly uncertain and disrupted environment, preventing them from reaching any stable identity or realizing their aspirations. The upheavals affecting international relations today, particularly under the influence of globalization disrupting rites and habits, make the rise of such postures easier than ever. Some people consider them to be 'madness' and others to be a permanent source of anxiety and uncertainty, disastrously undermining institutions: but they are also sources of innovations that never cease to surprise governments as well as all right-thinking people.

This situation is spreading more and more in the global world, favouring a growing pressure of social dynamics that run ahead of politics and cross borders, giving rise to those creative instabilities that escape the control of princes. Their names are populism, social anger, riots, resistance, transnational mobilizations, and so on: they make specialists in international relations uncomfortable, as they remain trapped in their old grammars when they should allow those new unstable situations to guide them in new research. These dynamic instabilities spread new themes that these 'mobilizations from below' ooze as they circulate spontaneously from one country to the next under the impact, in particular, of social networks, rapidly flooding the international agenda to the great dismay of princes who often fear them: ecology, respect for ethnic and sexual minorities, gender issues and the fight against all these forms of social differentiation, even 'intersectionality', the mere mention of which is almost criminalized in the most conservative circles.[7]

The fact remains that this *creative inscrutability* is gradually becoming a key concept in international relations, reshaping them and also triggering in its wake more traditional demands (democracy, disarmament, national emancipation, etc.). It is worth noting, for example, the rapid effect of the globalization of the #MeToo movement (starting in the United States in 2007, but affecting the entire world, in particular the Arab Spring and the Palestinian movement, as revealed in Maysaloun Hamoud's film *In Between*, released in 2017) and in Black Lives Matter (starting in 2013, globalizing very quickly and expanding to all forms of postcolonial denunciation): it is clear why they have flooded across the whole world and gradually formed common ground with wider causes, acting as chain reactions defying the usual conceptual frameworks of specialists in international relations.[8] Defying the traditional values linked to European history, they mobilize subjectively against the constructed international order and have a dramatic new impact on the relationships associated with it, triggering anew, often in a provocative manner, the global battle for norms. Even more, they in turn arouse conservative tensions exploited by certain authoritarian diplomacies, witness Putin, who denounces a 'depraved West' which, he claims, has turned paedophilia into 'the norm' (23 February 2023). Subjective impulses create a battle over meaning, thus nourishing traditional strategies.

The confusion of contexts

The old realist theory postulates, in the same vein, the objective nature of international contexts, which probably made sense in the past when societies were far from the international field and when princes – who had a quasi-monopoly – belonged 'to the same world'. Today, and as we have already seen, there is little chance that the globalized game that we play will lead to a common perception of the context in which states and people act. Western diplomacy has neglected the fact that the BRICS and the Global South understood the Ukrainian war not primarily as a violation of international law by Russia but as a settling of scores between the old powers of the North, if not as a Russian resistance to the Western hegemony embodied by NATO. The master of the Kremlin, more cunning on this point, took advantage of this, transforming his military defeats into diplomatic victories with a neglected Global South. Likewise, the French state interprets the conflict in the Sahel by confining it to the context of the 'global fight against jihadist terrorism', while local populations experience it as the expression of a desperate fight against a threefold breakdown – institutional, economic and social. It is not the same conflict in each case: this dissonance gives rise not only to misunderstandings but also to disastrous over-interpretations of the roles of each side and their goals.

Thus, the subjective reconstruction of contexts by each partner becomes an essential stage in research, as well as in the production of foreign policies. It presupposes that close attention be paid to the mode of description that each actor gives of their international environment, and above all a critique of the concepts used by the protagonists: the simple word 'terrorism' thus combines a reference to a mode of operation, to an organization (or even to several organizations, the competition between which is hidden), to local tactics, to a postulated international strategy, perhaps to a culture and a religion. Faced with this, a reference to vendetta, predation or individual insecurity suggests, among the other actors involved, completely different meanings that can never coincide with those of their opposite numbers, whether allies or enemies.

The war in Syria reveals the same blurring of meaning: the Russians intervene by resorting to traditional thought patterns, where power rivalries and windfall effects are combined, thus allowing them to extend their sphere of influence, and where a traditional geopolitical reading more or less shared by Western governments is required. On the other hand, Turkey and Iran perceive, in the same conflict, something completely different: a regional space in which are combined their desire to be recognized as predominant actors and a subtle play of complex and often contradictory transnational, ethnic and religious affinities. As for the Syrian internal forces, they understand the same event as an internal and social struggle directed against the authoritarian power of the Assad dynasty. This divergence of meaning results, in the apprehension of the same context, from incompatible readings, according to which games of alliance and connivance do not have the same meaning, are subject to fluctuations and are constantly reconstructed by all the parties involved. The enemy of my enemy is not always my friend: the Kurds are indeed the enemy of the Baathist regime, itself antagonistic to Turkey, but they are not for all that friends of the Turks. The friend of my friend is not necessarily my friend either, and the enemy of my friend is no longer mechanically my enemy ... These now 'tiered' wars no longer align meanings in a frontal and dual manner.

All these elements confirm that, contrary to prejudices, globalization does not erase local knowledge but, on the contrary, gives it enhanced relevance. The error, especially among those who claim hegemony on the world stage, is to believe in the homogenization of situations and to impose their order and their science as the measure of all things: perhaps this is why the old powers – who once alone set the standards for international relations – have been so commonly defeated since 1945, partly due to lack of understanding by those who were not members of the club. Perhaps this is also the reason for the rise in importance of transnational organizations, particularly borderless NGOs, precisely because they do not seek to import their own meanings to manage their relations with local populations.

Diplomacy has many meanings

In this new, complicated context, the art of diplomacy is always to 'manage separations', in the famous formula of the political scientist Paul Sharp: in its traditional version, it unfortunately gave little room for 'separations of meaning' even though, as we have seen, they underlay the most irreducible conflicts; on the contrary, it sought to maintain at all costs the illusion of a universal meaning, a natural extension of the culture that each person embodies. But does this major instrument already embody the same meaning in all cases? Yesterday, when it was wielded by the uniform plenipotentiaries of each prince, this simple form of diplomacy has become, in the era of globalization, complex and sometimes even confused. The bilateral relationship between similar princes naturally favoured negotiation, especially since it mobilized the same repertoire, based in a consensual manner on the relationship of power and on the transaction between presumed national interests. What was then self-evident and routine now becomes a permanent enigma that research must interpret and that action must overcome.

The increasingly subtle games of alliance initially complicated the traditional dyadic relationship. Thus the last two world wars resulted in a negotiation between the victors alone, busily managing the muddles of their coalition while excluding the defeated partners. The rise of multilateralism added to the complexity, since it was supposed to establish, at least partially, reference to a mysterious 'international community' in place of the easy paradigm of national interest: the result was often limited or even disappointing, with the sovereign state accepting the hypothesis of 'global governance' which sought to impose itself quietly, as revealed by the stalling of COPs on the climate question, where an impossible transaction regularly prevails over the need to regulate the system. Overall, the superposition of languages confuses the international game.

The current situation is aggravating the gap. The collapse of bipolarity has reinforced the fragmentation, even the illegibility, of positions: the idea of a lasting alliance is losing meaning outside the Western world, and institutionalized multilateralism does not really benefit from it. On the other hand, largely new forms of diplomacy are tending to appear, especially in the new world of Africa and Asia which has never been a home to the Westphalian system that was known only for the domination it formerly exercised to its detriment. Pragmatic modes of regional construction (such as the SCO, the Shanghai Cooperation Organization, with its Eurasian profile and loose internal ties) or of regional cooperation (such as the RCEP, the Regional Comprehensive Economic Partnership, a free trade zone in East Asia that brings together political rivals such as China, South Korea, Japan and Australia) are proliferating, leading astray a diplomatic game which is now far from uniform and conveys multiple meanings that do not fit together well.

The game becomes complicated when Western powers believe they can oppose these players with a traditional frontal model, such as the 'Indo-Pacific strategy' put forward by the French in the *White Paper for Security and National Defence* of 2013 and by the Americans in Joe Biden's speech of 21 October 2021.[9] There is a risk that the gap will remain permanent, unless it is overcome by the rigour of a renewed analysis. After a moment of hope aroused by the idea of universal socialization based on a common model of diplomacy operated by international institutions,[10] the decodification resulting from the collapse of bipolarity seems to have called everything into question, thus requiring a serious conceptual reordering.

But there is more at stake here: we face a real dilemma. *Either* negotiation is constructed 'the old-fashioned way' and often outside the real world, pre-empting the partners and ignoring all or some of the social parameters as well as the new actors on the ground – in which case its success in practice is very limited, witness the Oslo Accord (1993 on Palestine), or the agreements of Doha (2021, on Afghanistan), or even of Arusha (1993, on Rwanda), Abuja (1995, on Liberia), Algiers (1995, on Mali), Abidjan (1996, on Sierra Leone), and Libreville (2008 and 2013, on the Central African Republic). *Or* negotiation takes into account the data of the new conflictuality and then borders on aporia, since it must invite very diverse actors, state-based or not, whose rationalities are often contradictory, distinct cultures and referents, and whose very interest in negotiating is sometimes questionable; it must also take into consideration the social appropriation of the stakes, and in particular the change in meaning in the very idea of territory, which was once an easy basis for smooth negotiations but has now become a socially constructed common good which princes can no longer rely on controlling freely. These are all questions that should belong to the new grammar of princes and that societies have already made their own. And there are also questions of a semantic nature that research must place at the top of its agenda.

The semantic clash of powers

Likewise, power was once a unanimously adopted consensus, a key concept in international relations and a focal point of any action in foreign policy. It has now become, for similar reasons, a theme of division and debate[11] – not only between schools or as a subject for dissertations, but above all because it now bears different meanings: it is now at the confluence of three meanings, which clash in ways that now customarily drive the contemporary international game, to the point of making it a key question of new international relations. The traditional meaning remains, of course, linked to the capacity of a state to constrain all those who escape its sovereignty: here the military instrument is dominant without being exclusive. A second meaning makes the opposite wager, as it were, reinforced by the successful effects of social resistance opposed to the conquerors of yesterday: this 'power of the weak' mixes resistance and nuisance value to challenge the old levels of power. The third – which flourishes with globalization – reveals itself as systemic, as another capacity: that of controlling or conditioning the functioning of the global scene in order to derive maximum benefits from it.

It is easy to understand that each of these meanings corresponds, if not to a culture, at least to a history. The first corresponds to the European and North American tradition, in a lineage of interstate practice that goes from Machiavelli to Clausewitz via Hobbes, and reached its zenith during the Cold War. Stalled by decolonization and globalization, it has persisted through an effect of tradition, of course, but also through the relentless game of the 'fascination–hatred' pairing already noted, which has led many countries in the non-Western world to imitate it, or even to fight it. Just as Madame de Staël took pains to remind us, Napoleon's fiercest enemies never stopped admiring him in silence! This means that traditional power itself already assumes, through its origin and its destiny, several constantly evolving meanings which in turn collide.

For its part, 'power-resistance' is spreading among the weakest, while competing precisely with persistent and often disappointed hopes of making old-fashioned power their own. It elicits new forms and models of heroism, from Gandhi to Guevara – sources of a new international conquest of hearts and minds, combining the a priori antagonistic ideas of victor and martyr, as if the latter now more effectively drove the international agenda, shelving the traditional idea of victory as historically outdated.[12] It is significant that this inversion was entirely subject to the perception and subjectivity of an increasingly powerful public opinion in the Global South, where it provided new resources for revenge. The old powers then reacted by imposing a process of delegitimization, striving to push these new forms into the infamous category of 'terrorism', which is hardly understandable outside of their home countries.

As for systemic power, it wagers on the growing ineffectiveness of traditional warfare and the possibility of dominating without having to fight a battle, thus taking up the precept of the Chinese strategist Sun Tzu, who, as early as the sixth century BC, postulated that the best war was the war that could be won without having to fight it: in his view, the most efficacious factors were psychological action, the diversification of resources, yesterday's espionage and today's intelligence. This Chinese lineage, *inter alia*, provides the Asian empire with a significant advantage, as we can see in concrete today: we can also understand the particularity of the meaning that Beijing gives to the power game and the difficulty of Western partners to compete on this territory. In a globalized context, the power of the Other always has this indecipherable aspect, or at least an aspect that is not reducible to any one partner's categories, leading to an effect of surprise and ... helplessness. The gladiatorial game described by Hobbes once left little room for uncertainty: the new game – which is now the norm in our international relations – is much more difficult to decipher and therefore to anticipate, in analysis as well as in action, since the subjective factors are so heavy and diversified. We relied for too long on the reputedly solid compass that was supposed to define a priori what the national interest of each country was and the way in which it 'coloured' and animated geopolitics. Voluntary or not, the illusion was total. On the one hand, there never was an objective national interest specific to each country, but a subjective interpretation that each political entrepreneur gave it, in accordance with his own aims. On the other hand, it is becoming more and more scandalous that one can think of national interests other than as preconditioned by the global interest of the planet and of humanity as a whole – interests that we refuse to see: hence the urgency of working on the connection, as *thought* by each actor, of these two levels of daily international reality. The pressure of meaning in Europe and in the Sahel and Afghanistan, in Ukraine and in Vietnam, then trumps the performances formerly attributed to power and to yesterday's international practices as a whole. Mutual understanding thereby moves into the centre of the strategic sphere which was not used to welcoming it and which is disoriented, so to speak, by its irruption: neglecting it in analysis as in action will inevitably lead to failure.

A Tentative Conclusion: The Looming Battles for Meaning

Taking into account this entire subjective dimension of international relations leads to the undermining of many false ideas that have been taken for granted. This should encourage a diplomacy whose effectiveness depends more than ever on modesty and discretion, those two essential virtues, once we have become convinced that the incessant and lucid quest for an enigmatic otherness must prevail over the dogmatic desire to appear in the 'front row' and to assert one's 'special responsibilities'. The old hierarchical posture, in a globalized world, merely arouses distrust and hostility while being based on an outdated and inoperative order: thus, it can lead only to failure. This outmoded diplomacy, self-evident in any objective reading in terms of 'balance of power', appears fragile and costly to a subjective approach. This is where the challenge lies: to move from a world dominated by verticality to another with a new, horizontal configuration!

This observation is also an invitation to discover the real complexity that now obtains: the international

A Tentative Conclusion

game, as we have seen, is made up of two curious intersections, combining objective data that have not disappeared, such as the tensions aroused in matters of energy policies, with increasingly pressing subjective parameters that have always been marginalized. Likewise, the Hobbesian dream of a uniform international arena, exclusively reserved for state gladiators, 'diplomats and soldiers', has not disappeared but needs to coexist with a globalized scene, confronted with a number of new issues: the economy, health, the climate, and social matters that deserve better than the pompous and pious interstate rhetoric crafted by masters of communication who completely fail to address the new issues at stake.

The knowledge that we must construct to decipher this new world does not necessarily involve a composite epistemology, a patchwork of concepts from different horizons. The first paradox we have stated in no way rescues the positivism of yesteryear: if objective, geographical, historical and economic parameters naturally continue to weigh on the international order, they can only act through the actors who interpret them, give them a meaning and choose to get by with them. This permanent deliberation on our familiar environment cancels all of the transcendent pretensions of geopolitics and annihilates its so-called laws. Indeed, it reveals the fragility of the very notion of national interest, a common fetish in diplomatic and strategic discourse: there is no objective national interest, but only the individual *representation* by the actors involved of what is for them the interest of the nation they lead or to which they belong. This representation then operates more as a mode of legitimization of their choices than as a pri-

A Tentative Conclusion

mary guide to their own political or strategic options. Worse still, while claiming to be realistic, it leads one into the perilous spheres of a past world which ignores the demands of globality.

In the same way, the duality of scenes – one scene that animates the conformist imagination of princes and another that results from this international social activism – does not imply two separate approaches. If the concepts of the old realism are obviously useful for understanding how leaders' actions are organized, they do not account for the failure which results from their unsuitable strategy. It is by spreading the influence of realism, integrating it into a broader sociological approach, understanding the active exchange between the two scenes, focusing on their interactive nature – the way in which one distorts the other – that one can move forward in the analysis. It is the failures of the old strategy of conquest inspired by a past world that led Vladimir Putin to rely on these new parameters which until then had seemed secondary to him; thus it was that he exploited economic and social partitions and, more quickly than his adversaries, espoused a new diplomacy that broke away from old ideas of alliance and surfed along on subjective parameters such as humiliation, resentment, fear of Western hegemony and the inversion of values.

These practices seek out the human dimension even beyond structures, unfortunately even if this means manipulating and transfiguring it: 'battles for meaning' will occupy the international sphere for a long time. Being aware of this allows us to keep up with our times, avoid dead ends and disappointments, give ourselves a chance of success, and finally achieve a positive peace.

A Tentative Conclusion

This is quite something – but malevolence can also exploit it to take its revenge. The battle over meanings lies at the centre of the global game: to ignore this battle means that we lose it; taking it into account does not mean that we can be sure of winning it. Suffice it to say, contrary to legendary naivety, that History is never finished.

Notes

Preface
1 Bertrand Badie, *Vivre deux cultures: Comment peut-on naître franco-persan?* (Paris: Odile Jacob, 2022).

Introduction
1 The French writer Prosper Mérimée composed a fiendishly difficult dictation which he gave as a form of entertainment to the court of Napoleon III at Fontainebleau in 1857 (Translator's note).
2 Here and elsewhere, Badie uses the term 'princes' to refer, as is standard in a certain kind of historical discourse, to rulers, even if they were not royal (Translator's note).
3 Friedrich Schleiermacher, *Hermeneutics and Criticism and Other Writings*, trans. Andrew Bowie (Cambridge: Cambridge University Press, 1998).
4 Pyotr Chaadayev, *Lettres philosophiques*, vol. I (Paris: La République des Lettres, [1828] 2020).

5 Françafrique is a term used to refer to France's continuing influence in French-speaking Africa (especially its former colonies) (Translator's note).
6 Paul Sharp, *Diplomatic Theory of International Relations* (Cambridge: Cambridge University Press, 2012).
7 Bertrand Badie, *Humiliation in International Relations: A Pathology of Contemporary International Systems*, trans. Jeff Lewis (London: Bloomsbury, 2017).
8 Delphine Allès, Sonia Le Gouriellec and Mélissa Levaillant (eds), *Paix et sécurité: Une anthologie décentrée* (Paris: Éditions du CNRS, 2023).
9 Alexander Wendt, *Social Theory of International Politics* (Cambridge: Cambridge University Press, 1999); Nicholas Onuf, *World of Our Making. Rules and Rule in Social Theory and International Relations* (London: Routledge, 1989).
10 Hans-Georg Gadamer, *Truth and Method*, 2nd edn, trans. rev. Joel Weinsheimer and Donald G. Marshall (London: Bloomsbury, 2004).
11 George Kennan, *Russia and the War under Lenin and Stalin* (Boston: Little, Brown, 1961).
12 Gary King, Robert Keohane and Sidney Verba, *Designing Social Inquiry* (Princeton, NJ: Princeton University Press, 1994), p. 15.
13 Elizabeth Grosz, *The Nick of Time: Politics, Evolution, and the Untimely* (Durham, NC: Duke University Press, 2004).
14 Morgan Brigg and Roland Bleiker, 'Autoethnographic international relations: the self as a source of knowledge', *Review of International Studies*, 36 (2010): 779–95 (at p. 789).

Chapter 1 The Return of Geopolitics

1 Harold James, 'Geopolitics is for losers', *Aeon*, 1 December 2022, https://aeon.co/essays/geopolitics-is-a-losers-buzzword-with-a-contagious-idea (p. 4).
2 Friedrich Ratzel, *Politische Geographie* (Munich and Leipzig: Oldenbourg, 1997).
3 James, 'Geopolitics is for losers'.
4 Ibid., p. 8.
5 Karl Haushofer, *Wehr-Geopolitik: Geographische Grundlagen einer Wehrkunde* (Berlin: Junker & Dünnhaupt, 1941).
6 Émile Durkheim, 'Compte rendu de Friedrich Ratzel, Anthropogéographie', *L'Année sociologique*, 1899, section 6: 'Morphologie sociale, I: Les migrations humaines', http://classiques.uqac.ca/classiques/Durkheim_emile/ratzel_anthropo_geographie/ratzel_anthropo_geo.html.
7 Bernard Valade, 'Enjeux disciplinaires: Émile Durkheim et Friedrich Ratzel', in Raymond Boudon (ed.), *Durkheim fut-il durkheimien? Actes du colloque organisé les 4 et 5 novembre 2008 par l'Académie des sciences morales et politiques* (Paris: Armand Colin, 2011), pp. 41–54.
8 Fred Kaplan, 'Henry Kissinger wrote a peace plan for Ukraine. It's ludicrous', *Slate*, 16 December 2022.
9 John M. Collins, *Grand Strategy: Principles and Practices* (Annapolis, MD: Naval Institute Press, 1973); John Lewis Gaddis, *On Grand Strategy* (London: Penguin, 2018).
10 Carl Schmitt, *The Concept of the Political*, trans. George Schwab (Chicago: University of Chicago Press, 1996).

11 Hans Morgenthau, *Politics among Nations* (New York: Knopf, 1948).
12 Olivier Dollfus, *La Mondialisation*, 3rd edn (Paris: Presses de Sciences Po, 2007).
13 Jacques Lévy, 'Beyond geopolitics: a French connection', in Jacques Lévy (ed.), *From Geopolitics to Global Politics* (London: Frank Cass, 2000), pp. 1–6.
14 Gearóid Ó Tuathail, *Critical Geopolitics: The Politics of Writing Global Space* (Minneapolis: University of Minnesota Press, 1996).
15 Ibid., p. 12.
16 Lévy, 'Beyond geopolitics', p. 5.
17 Ibid., p. 2.

Chapter 2 The Two International Scenes and Their Multiple Meanings

1 Barry Buzan and Richard Little (eds), *International Systems in World History: Remaking the Study of International Relations* (Oxford: Oxford University Press, 2000).
2 Dipesh Chakrabarty, *Provincializing Europe: Postcolonial Thought and Historical Difference*, new edn (Princeton, NJ: Princeton University Press, 2007).
3 Arthur Jay Klinghoffer, *The Power of Projections: How Maps Reflect Global Politics and History* (Westport, CT: Praeger, 2006).
4 Andrew Linklater and Hidemi Suganami, *The English School of International Relations* (Cambridge: Cambridge University Press, 2006), pp. 144ff.
5 Hedley Bull, *The Anarchical Society* (London: Palgrave, [1977] 2002).

6 Ji Zhe, '*Tianxia*, retour en force d'un concept oublié', *La Vie des idées*, 3 December 2008, https://laviedesidees.fr/Tianxia-retour-en-force-d-un; Wang Gungwu and Zheng Yongnian (eds), *China and the New International Order* (London: Routledge, 2008); Yongnian Zheng and Dan Wu, 'Wang Gungwu and the study of China's international relations', in Niv Horesh and Emilian Kavalski (eds), *Asian Thought on China's Changing International Relations* (London: Palgrave, 2014), pp. 54–75.
7 Tingyang Zhao, *Tianxia, tout sous un même ciel* (Paris: Le Cerf, 2018).
8 Ibid.
9 Zheng and Wu, 'Wang Gungwu and the study of China's international relations', p. 63.
10 John Fairbank (ed.), *The Chinese World Order: Traditional China's Foreign Relations* (Cambridge, MA: Harvard University Press, 1968).

Chapter 3 Four Questions That Have Become Fundamental

1 Voltaire, *Candide*, www.gutenberg.org/cache/epub/19942/pg19942-images.html.
2 Gary Olson, 'Clifford Geertz on ethnography and social construction', *Journal of Advanced Composition*, 11/2 (1991): 245–68.
3 Richard Rorty, *Philosophy and the Mirror of Nature* (Princeton, NJ: Princeton University Press, 1979).
4 Stanley Hoffmann, *Gulliver's Troubles: Or, the Setting of American Foreign Policy* (New York: McGraw-Hill, 1968).
5 Wilhelm Dilthey, *Die geistige Welt: Einleitung in die Philosophie des Lebens. Erste Hälfte: Abhandlungen*

zur Grundlegung der Geisteswissenschaften, ed. Georg Misch (Leipzig: B. G. Teubner, 1914); Guillaume Fagniez, 'Dilthey et les catégories de la vie', *Les Études philosophiques*, 122/3 (2017): 385–400.

6 Philip Quincy Wright, *A Study of War* (Chicago: University of Chicago Press, 1942).

7 Peter Berger, 'Identity as a problem in the sociology of knowledge', *European Journal of Sociology*, 7/1 (1966): 105–15.

8 Quoted in Philippe Humbert, *Des Indes au Brexit, l'imaginaire impérial de Winston Churchill*, Fondation Jean-Jaurès, 24 January 2021; www.jean-jaures.org/publication/des-indes-au-brexit-limaginaire-imperial-de-winston-churchill/.

9 Alistair Johnston, *Social States: China in International Institutions, 1980–2000* (Princeton, NJ: Princeton University Press, 2008).

10 Alistair Johnston and Mingming Shen (eds), *Perception and Misperception in American and Chinese Views of the Other* (Washington, DC: Carnegie Endowment for International Peace, 2015).

11 Alex Mintz, 'How do leaders make decisions? A poliheuristic perspective', *Journal of Conflict Resolution*, 48/1 (2004): 3–13.

12 Wioletta Miskiewicz, 'Vers un fondement psychologique transcendantal des sciences', *Methodos*, 2 (2002); https://philpapers.org/rec/MISVUF.

13 Gary Goertz, *Contexts of International Politics* (Cambridge: Cambridge University Press, 1994).

14 Graham Allison, *Destined for War: Can America and China Escape Thucydides' Trap?* (Boston: Mariner Books, 2017).

15 Nicholas Onuf, *World of Our Making: Rules and Rule in Social Theory and International Relations* (London: Routledge, 1989).
16 Gabriel Almond and Stephen Genco, 'Clouds, clocks, and the study of politics', *World Politics*, 29/4 (1977): 489–522.
17 Nirad Chaudhuri, *The Autobiography of an Unknown Indian* (Berkeley, CA: University of California Press, [1951] 1969).
18 David Mitrany, *A Working Peace System: An Argument for the Functional Development of International Organization* (London: Royal Institute of International Affairs; New York: Oxford University Press, 1943); Guillaume Devin, 'Que reste-t-il du fonctionnalisme international? Relire David Mitrany (1888–1975)', *Critique internationale*, 38/1 (2008): 137–52; Kofi Annan, with Nader Mousavizadeh, *Interventions: A Life in War and Peace* (London: Penguin, 2013), pp. 227ff.

Chapter 4 Rethinking the International Agenda

1 Mattias Iser, 'Recognition between states? Moving beyond identity politics', in Christopher Daase et al. (eds), *Recognition in International Relations* (London: Palgrave, 2015), pp. 27–48.
2 Joel Birman and Claudine Haroche, 'Avant-propos: Le besoin d'essentiel', in Georges Balandier (ed.), *Le Dépaysement contemporain: L'essentiel et l'immédiat. Entretiens avec Joël Birman et Claudine Haroche* (Paris: Presses Universitaires de France, 2009), pp. 1–11.

3 Operation Barkhane was a counter-insurgency operation (2014–22) by the French army against Islamist groups in the Sahel.
4 Joseph Nye, *Soft Power: The Means to Success in World Politics* (New York: Public Affairs, 2004); Frédéric Charillon, *Guerres d'influence: Les États à la conquête des esprits* (Paris: Odile Jacob, 2002).
5 Max Scheler, *Ressentiment*, ed. Lewis A. Coser, trans. William W. Holdheim (New York: Schocken, 1972).
6 Helmuth Plessner, 'De homine abscondito', *Social Research*, 36 (1969): 497–509; Helmuth Plessner, *The Levels of Organic Life and the Human: Introduction to Philosophical Anthropology*, trans. Millay Hyatt (New York: Fordham University Press, 2019); Hans-Peter Krüger, 'L'expressivité comme fondement de l'historicité future', *Trivium*, 25 (2017), https://journals.openedition.org/trivium/5483.
7 Naysan Adlparvar and Mariz Tadros, 'The evolution of ethnicity: theory, intersectionality, geopolitics and development', *IDS Bulletin*, 47/2 (2006): 123–36; Kalpana Wilson, *Race, Racism and Development: Interrogating History, Discourse and Practice* (London: Zed Books, 2012).
8 Gaëlle Gillot and Andrea Martinez, *Femmes, Printemps arabes et revendications citoyennes* (Paris: IRD, 2016); Bertrand Tillier, *La Disgrâce des statues: Essai sur les conflits de mémoires, de la Révolution française à Black Lives Matter* (Paris: Payot, 2022).
9 US Department of State, 2022, 'Fact sheet: Indo-Pacific strategy of the United States', www.white

house.gov/briefing-room/speeches-remarks/2022/02/11/fact-sheet-indo-pacific-strategy-of-the-united-states/.
10 Jeffrey Checkel, *International Institutions and Socialization*, ARENA working paper, University of Oslo, 1989; Guillaume Devin, *Les Organisations internationales* (Paris: Armand Colin, 2022), pp. 139–42.
11 Bertrand Badie, *Les Puissances mondialisées* (Paris: Odile Jacob, 2021).
12 Gaïdz Minassian, *Les Sentiers de la victoire: Peut-on encore gagner une guerre?* (Paris: Passés composés, 2020).